MW00423699

UNLEASHING THE POWER OF PRAYING IN THE SPIRIT!

by Oral Roberts

Unless otherwise indicated,
all Scripture quotations are from
the King James Version of the Bible.

Copyright © 1993
by Oral Roberts
Tulsa, Oklahoma 74171

BK 643

TABLE OF CONTENTS

INTRODUCTION

Oh, it's a glorious thing when a human being is saved by the blood of Jesus, born again by the Holy Spirit, becomes a new creature in Christ and begins his thrilling new walk with the Lord. And I believe the first and foremost desire that comes into the heart of every believer is to enter *the realm of the miraculous.* Every child of God has a longing in his spirit to follow Jesus, his Savior, into that realm where the miracles are, where the wind of the Spirit blows ceaselessly — that realm of the invisible where angels move in multiplied millions as ministers for his redemption.

It is there, just beyond our natural eyesight, that our faith connects with the unseen world which surrounds us, and in that supernatural realm we can use our faith to tap into the miracles that brought Jesus Christ into this earth as our Lord and Savior. It's in the unseen realm where the Holy Spirit operates as the unlimited presence of Jesus and where the Lord Himself is now seated at the Father's right hand. And in this invisible world, from which we're separated only by the veil of our humanness, believers have access *every moment* to the miraculous — to the miracle life which our salvation from sin has bought for us!

How can we penetrate the invisible and reach that supernatural realm of God? ***It's by the power of His Spirit!*** I'll tell you, the Lord wants His people to be MIRACLE PEOPLE! He wants us to plug in to the miraculous through the unlimited power of His Spirit! He wants to give us a Holy Ghost rain of His power — not a trickle, not a stream, not a river, but a MIGHTY TORRENT! What we need is an earth-moving, gully-washing rain from Heaven, a spiritual rain that will make Noah's flood look like dew!

This whole world needs a sin-busting, devil-casting-out, sickness-healing HOLY GHOST OUTPOURING from the throne room of God in Heaven! For with Holy Ghost power flowing through our lives we'll enter that realm where the miracles are! And with the power that spins the universe bursting from our hearts, ***WE'LL DO GREAT EXPLOITS FOR OUR GOD!***

Chapter 1

A TALKING GOD AND A TALKING PERSON

"Oral, you've got to pray," Mamma whispered as I lay deathly ill with tuberculosis, 14 years before the antibiotic drugs were discovered which would have driven this dreaded disease out of my body. "Son, you've got to talk to God!" she exclaimed, big tears rolling down her cheeks, but with a strong set to her jaw.

Sound simple? Maybe so, in today's world, with much more being grasped and understood about prayer. Today I understand the very real possibility of a human being (no matter what his circumstances) actually talking to God and then hearing the Lord speak back to him in his soul. But it wasn't that simple to me back then.

After all, I had never seen God. It's hard in the world you and I live in, a world of terrible and dark reality, of hurt and illness and grief and death, to even contemplate a Being that seems to be so vague and incomprehensible as God. Oh, He was so faraway, so abstract to me, that I thought, *Who am*

I, Oral Roberts, a stuttering, stammering boy, born among the hills of Oklahoma . . . who am I to talk to God?

Besides, talking to God definitely implied that He would talk to me, and that was more than my mind could fathom as I lay there on my bed at the end of five cruel months of a terminal illness . . . hacking, coughing, hemorrhaging, holding on but knowing I was probably going to die at age 17 1/2 . . . before I had even had a chance to live.

Like the meteors streaking across the heavens and landing in unknown places, Mamma's words, "You've got to pray . . . talk to God," streaked through my consciousness with no more reality than the meteors exploding into bits somewhere out in the atmosphere — out of sight, out of mind.

But, somehow, in spite of my feverish stupor, Mamma's words struck a chord in me that slowly but surely began the music of my life that still rings in my soul today. And, finally, I got the point. In that fleeting instant, something caused me to cry out: "How, Mamma, how?" I didn't have the slightest idea how to pray!

I knew that Mamma and Papa knew how to pray, and I had a vague sense that there were a few others I knew who also did. But me? Talking to God seemed so far-fetched and improbable that I had almost no hope of ever breaking through the mystery of it.

10

I had no concept of praying, no notion of how to talk to God. But Mamma was Mamma and she looked at me with a look so piercing it was like she was looking straight through me. Her dark brown eyes (denoting her Cherokee Indian blood) spoke louder than her words, pleading with me to pray, to talk to God.

She and Papa, my preacher father, had shed many tears over my life, but they had never lied to me or tried to fool me. They were straight shooters and always tender toward me, being the baby of the family, and my two brothers and sister. Besides, Mamma wouldn't have been telling me to pray as I lay there deathly ill, wasting away to skin and bones, had she not believed that I could and should talk to God — and that He would hear and answer the prayer of a stuttering, stammering boy's heart.

She didn't say anything more at that time beyond those few priceless words, and neither did I. <u>Little did I know that she had planted a seed and that seed was buried deep in the soil of my heart.</u> Nor did I ever dream that soon, very soon, that seed would germinate when Papa walked into my room one night and announced bluntly, but ever so kindly, "Oral, you've got to be saved. You've got to believe in Jesus. Son, you must not go to hell. You must go to Heaven when you die!"

You see, I was so far gone, with the blood pouring out of my body through hemorrhaging, that

11

even Papa had little hope that I would live. Mamma always believed God would heal me, but Papa's great burden was for me to be saved before I died. And by that time, the road I was walking was so blurred that I really didn't know which it was going to be! I was caught between two worlds as the fever and the knifelike pains wracked my body, and yet my mind was drifting further and further away, making God seem even more "unreal" to me.

I remember how Mamma and the nurse came into my room that night and sat down by my bedside. Mamma had emerged from the kitchen with her apron still wrapped around her waist, and I saw her pull it up in front of her face to cover her eyes, which were bursting with tears. The nurse who had been sitting with me for several weeks was weeping softly at Mamma's side.

Papa cleared his throat and then he declared with his strong, deep voice, "Oral, this is it for you, for us your parents and family, for all who love you. Tonight I'm going to kneel and pray and I'm not getting off my knees until you get saved and are right with God before you die."

But as a young boy lying there upon the bed of affliction, I had no desire to go to Heaven at all . . . *I JUST WANTED TO LIVE!*

My head was reeling as Papa's words rang in my ears. You see, Papa carried his own "public address" system in that powerful voice of his, and the sound of his words filled up that little room! I'll never forget how he knelt at the foot of my bed and rose up on his knees and, oh, he was letting it out as he told the Lord about his son, Oral Roberts!

> **HOW FORTUNATE IS THE PERSON WHO HAS SOMEONE TO HOLD THE ROPE FOR THEM LIKE PAPA AND MAMMA HELD THE ROPE FOR ME!**

When I look back at that fateful night, I can still hear in my mind many of the words Papa said to God, not that I could see God or even grasp that He was out there somewhere. But Papa talked as if He were right there in the room with us, not in some distant realm or shapeless form. To Papa, God was the most real Person he had ever known and, ever since I had been old enough to understand anything at all, I had heard Papa talk to God.

I was blessed by being born into a home where my father felt the call of God to preach and my mother believed in the healing power of the Lord. (She believed in divine healing more than anyone I had ever known in my life.) Mamma and Papa were dear and beloved parents. They loved me, they cared about me, and they taught me the way of the Lord. Oh, I'm glad I was born of Ellis Melvin Roberts and Claudius Priscilla Roberts, who breathed on me the breath of their faith!

MAMMA AND PAPA TALKED TO JESUS
LIKE HE LIVED AT OUR HOUSE

Now, my mother and father had been filled with the Holy Spirit before I was born and they spoke with tongues and magnified God. Why, they were so close to the Lord, and the Holy Ghost was such a powerful reality in their lives, that they would talk to Jesus like He actually lived at our house!

I have vivid memories of how, when we were boys, my brother Vaden and I would wake up around four o'clock in the morning, hearing Mamma and Papa talking. And many a night we would rise from our sleep when we heard them whispering and they were talking to Jesus. I really believed the Lord lived right there in our home with us! My friend, that's a very remarkable thought, because that's just how wonderful it is to have the power of the Holy Ghost in your life! *It's like having Jesus in the flesh living at your house!*

Why then couldn't I grasp what it meant when Mamma said to me, "Oral, you've got to pray . . . you've got to talk to God"? Certainly Papa's dedication that night to stay on his knees, praying and talking to God FOR ME until I came face to face with my relationship with Jesus Christ, should have meant something real and eminently personal to me. Sadly enough, it didn't!

It wasn't that I didn't believe in God. I lived with parents who loved Jesus . . . but I was totally indifferent. <u>I had grown up in a devoutly religious family, but I don't remember ever having had a single religious feeling in my life until that very night!</u>

You see, I lived in my own world, dreaming my own dreams and, in my own childlike way, I believed they might come true. My Grandfather Roberts had been a judge in Oklahoma during the Indian Territory days, and he was so dear to me that he had become the role model for my life. Perhaps that's why I wanted to be a lawyer so badly. I even dared to hope that someday I might be elected the governor of Oklahoma!

My grandfather was my hero and, in looking up to him, my own ambitions had become like great dazzling gods to me. Furthermore, I was firmly convinced that if I became a Christian, I could not attain my high-sounding ambitions. *Therefore, my dreams were standing in the way of my conversion!*

Now don't misunderstand what I'm saying. There was nothing wrong with my desire to become a lawyer, and even my childish dream of becoming governor of the state of Oklahoma was not wrong in itself. But the fact that I was consumed with doing something different with my life from what God had

15

planned for me was what was wrong. I was not inclined toward the Lord at all, or what He wanted for my life. <u>So even in the desperate extremity of my young life, praying and talking to God never seriously occurred to me.</u>

As my mind goes back to my youth and my running-away days, I remember how as a vibrant teenager I was totally absorbed with living life to the fullest. And, at the age of 16, I walked away from my mother and father to pursue the dreams that were burning in my heart. I not only left their home, but I abandoned their way of life and the God they loved and served. When I told them of my decision, Papa exclaimed, "Son, I'll put every policeman in Oklahoma on your trail! They will bring you back!"

"Yeah, and I'll run away again!" I snapped back at him. And I believe he knew my mind was made up, so Papa just let me go.

It's forever etched on my memory how, as I was leaving home, Mamma pulled me down close — she was only five feet tall and I was six feet, one inch — and she kissed me, and her tears splashed hotly on my cheeks. How I wished she wouldn't have said what she said next.

With her lip trembling, she whispered these words in my ear: "Oral, you may run away from us, but you will never run away from God. My prayers will track you down and bring you back home again!"

So I slammed the door on my family and walked out of that cotton patch into the wide world of my dreams.

Weeks and months flew by as I was grappling out in the world without God. I was working my way through high school while boarding in the home of a judge, and I was already tackling his law books on the side. Besides that, I was participating in one of the greatest thrills of my life — playing basketball. Ironically, it was in the midst of a district championship game that I collapsed on the court and began bleeding from my mouth. As I lapsed in and out of consciousness, I can remember my coach telling me, "*Oral, I'm taking you home now.*"

Then he stretched me out on the backseat of his car and we raced over those back roads to Ada, Oklahoma, where my parents lived. When my father's large frame appeared in the doorway, the coach exclaimed, "Reverend Roberts, I've brought your son home. Can you help me carry him in?" My mind was in a blur as they carried me into the house, hemorrhaging, coughing, hacking. They laid me on the bed and summoned our doctors.

After countless tests and diagnoses, they declared I had tuberculosis. Now, all at once, instead of being absorbed with my own grandiose dreams and ambitions, I was abruptly confronted with this terrible life-threatening infection which had settled upon my lungs.

You see, tuberculosis ran rampant among the American Indians of that day, and it's still a disease which is almost indigenous to the Indian people. Papa was a descendant of Welsh/Norse forefathers who had come to America in the early 1800s, and he had fallen in love with a pretty little Indian girl, Claudius Priscilla Irwin (her last name coming from her white father and her mother's maiden name being Holden). He married her in "the nations" of the Indian tribes of Oklahoma when he was 19 and she was 15.

Mamma's people died like flies with the white man's disease of tuberculosis and his poison of corn liquor. Even her white father had collapsed and died with tuberculosis at age 50, before I was born, and two of her sisters had perished with it before it finally fastened its deadly grip on me.

The disease operated almost like deadly witchcraft among the Indians. When you contracted tuberculosis, the people pronounced a death sentence on you, declaring, "He's going to die!" And this form of witchcraft was believed in and clung to as unquestionably as one's own breathing!

But, in the midst of that cruel, five-month period of being bedfast, hovering between life and death, here was Mamma telling me of a talking God and of me talking to Him . . . and somehow her words penetrated my spirit. I'm convinced I've got a story to tell that will take root in your mind and spirit in the same way as when I first heard Mamma whispering in my ear those priceless words, "Oral, you've got to talk to God."

I didn't come to grips with the Bible way of praying, of talking in "tongues" to God and then listening to "interpret" His response back to my mind, until much later. For when it's all said and done, and you get into the natural flow of it, this two-way praying can open up the realm of the miraculous in a way that nothing else can! ***And when a talking God and a talking person start talking to each other,*** **GREAT AND MIGHTY MIRACLES CAN HAPPEN.** And that thrilling revelation is what this book is really all about!

It's a mighty river flowing!

Chapter 2

TALKING DOESN'T START WITH YOUR TONGUE, BUT WITH YOUR BELLY

Do you know what the Lord Jesus Christ said about those of us who believe in Him? He declared, **"Out of his belly** shall flow rivers of living water. [But this spake he of the Spirit, which they that believe on him should receive: for the Holy Ghost was not yet given; because that Jesus was not yet glorified]" (John 7:38,39). The Lord described the Holy Ghost as a river, as a flood, as a welling up inside you, coming up out of your belly area and rolling over your tongue in "rivers of living water."

I have discovered that your belly area, which is called the solar plexus, is the most sensitive part of your being, not only in your anatomy but also in your spirit and mind. So it's not surprising that the Holy Spirit would indwell this most sensitive part of your anatomy and that from this source in your belly area a river more wonderful than words could begin to flow!

I used to believe I talked with my tongue

because that's the organ that formed the words and pushed them out of my mouth as sounds. But gradually it dawned on me that if this area in my belly — the source of my feelings — wasn't flowing, my tongue was only a bit of flesh in my mouth, dormant and inarticulate. <u>However, let life touch my inner being, which I feel in my solar plexus, and my tongue flips into motion without any conscious action on my part.</u>

Really, if you think about it, your tongue couldn't possibly be the source of your speech any more than a hydrant or the sprinkler in your backyard is where the water begins its flow. **THE WATER BEGINS TO FLOW WHEN THE PRESSURE COMING FROM THE *SOURCE* OF THE WATER THAT BUILDS UP BEHIND THE HYDRANT IS RELEASED WHEN YOU TURN THE HYDRANT ON.** *But you have to turn it on!*

TO REALLY HEAR THE LORD SPEAK, YOU MUST HAVE A LISTENING HEART

I grew up around the Bible, born into a home where my parents had a strong belief in the Word of God. Papa was a powerful preacher, a terrific communicator, but I still didn't know the Bible, even though I knew many of its words and could recite many passages from memory. The God of E. M. Roberts and Claudius Priscilla Roberts was not the God of Oral Roberts until **I** believed, and then God became the God of Oral Roberts.

Oh, I grew up going to Sunday school and church because Mamma and Papa commanded me to go, but I was still a very irreligious young man. I had heard all the sermons and the beautiful hymns, and sometimes a flash of something would filter down into my spirit, but most of the time nothing much penetrated my heart.

I believe there were times as a child when the Lord spoke to me, but somehow it didn't register on my consciousness that it was God, because I didn't have a listening heart, and I was not tuned in to listen to God.

> **I'LL TELL YOU, GOD WILL TALK TO YOU WHETHER YOU'RE CLOSE TO HIM OR FAR AWAY!**

Now, certainly, you can hear Him much more clearly if you're up close, but the point I want to drive home is this: *to really hear the Lord, you must have a listening heart.* You have to listen way down on the inside for the still, small voice of His Spirit.

Now I'm going to tell you a little story about God's talking and, every time I tell it, it absolutely breaks me up. It happened many years ago when my father was out preaching and our family had run

22

out of food. I remember how Mamma came down to the kitchen that evening around dinner time and there was literally nothing in the house to eat. "Boys, let's go visiting," she suggested, and, in spite of the empty feeling gnawing at the pit of our stomachs, we followed her out the door as she headed for the Campbell's house.

By the time we arrived, they were sitting down to supper and Sister Campbell exclaimed, "Oh, you're just in time to have supper."

But Mamma replied quickly, "Oh, no, we're not hungry."

About that time my brother Vaden, who was a year older than I was, rammed his elbow into my side and whispered hoarsely, "Boy, I wish she had asked me!"

As we sat there watching them eat that good country cooking, I don't know about Mamma, but Vaden and Oral were having a terrible time with their stomachs! After they had cleared away the last of the supper dishes, it was time for us to go home and Sister Campbell sighed, "Oh, Sister Roberts, before you go, let's pray." The next thing we knew, Mamma and Sister Campbell were down on their knees, praying up a storm! Really, I thought they were going to pray all night!

Pretty soon I heard Mamma declare, "O God, how good You are! What a good God You are, and how good You've been to us!"

Vaden rolled his eyes at me and punched me in the ribs again as he whispered, "He ain't been very good to me!"

Now Vaden was a good boy. I don't mean to insinuate that he wasn't. But that night as he and I shuffled our way home with Mamma, he was really working God over! He even blurted out what an awful thing Mamma had done, first of all, by not letting us eat when Sister Campbell had invited us, and then she had had the gall to pray that prayer about how good God is and how the Lord was meeting all our needs!

He was going on and on when, all at once, something rose up out of my belly area, words that just burst out of my being, and I piped up, *"Vaden, God will take care of us!"*

But he completely ignored me and kept on whining and sniveling, "Well, Papa's a preacher and he's gone all the time and people don't give him anything and we're always running out of food. Besides, we've never even owned an automobile!" And on and on and on he went.

Finally, I exclaimed in exasperation, "Vaden, you shut up! ***God will take care of us!***"

Now, I wasn't aware that that was God speaking to me. I wasn't thinking about God at all. Those words just popped out! They came bursting out of my innermost being, out of my belly! And, for a few fleeting seconds, <u>those words turned the Spirit of</u>

24

God on inside a boy named Oral Roberts!

When we reached the doorstep of our little house, Mamma said, "Vaden, open the door."

But when he tried to push the door open, he cried, "Mamma, there's something behind this door!" So he shoved with all of his might and, when he finally forced the door open and flipped on the light, there was the most gigantic box of groceries we had ever seen in our lives!

Well, Mamma didn't act like it was anything strange at all! In fact, she never even missed a stride as she told us, "Boys, put that box in the kitchen," and we began to dive in! There were all kinds of food in that box — great big sacks of flour and sugar and even a country ham!

Then Mamma exclaimed, "Bring me my apron!" and as she talked about the Lord being so good to us, she began slicing that ham and dumping flour and baking powder into a bowl to make homemade biscuits and cream gravy. I guess it was almost midnight when she finally spread that meal before us and we began shoveling it in — big hot biscuits, country ham, red-eye gravy and cream gravy!

I'll never forget how I sat there with my mouth full, a great big grin on my face, and I turned to Vaden and exclaimed triumphantly, ***"See! I told you God would take care of us!"***

Now, I didn't understand that that was God whispering in my ear as a little child, but there He was, speaking to me way back then. Time and time again things like that happened, but I never realized it was the Lord.

I DIDN'T HAVE THE SLIGHTEST IDEA THAT WORDS OR PRAYERS ORIGINATED IN MY BELLY AREA

On that fateful night when Papa announced at my bedside that he was going to kneel and talk to God about me and my condition until I came face to face with Christ and got saved, I hadn't the slightest idea that words or prayers originated in my belly area, the area where I feel my "inner man." Neither did I know that someone talking to God in my behalf could reach a place of such miraculous conversation with Him that it could spark something in this most sensitive area of my being and, in the sweep of a moment, I would be talking to God as if I had talked to Him every day, all my life!

Out of the corner of my eye I caught a glimpse of Mamma and the nurse rising from their knees as they finished praying and sat down by my bed. But Papa was still praying the way only preachers can and, really, it sounded as if he'd only just begun!

I could hear him without even glancing at his face. Dear me, you could have heard his powerful voice, now dealing with my very life, hundreds of feet away! Of course, since all my life I had heard

Papa pray or "talk to God," as he put it, there was nothing unusual to me about what he was doing. To be frank, I was paying very little attention to him. I was still so wrapped up in my own little world that it hadn't fully dawned on me how little of it I might actually have left on this earth!

All at once, the kind of spontaneous something that grabs your attention gripped my whole being and caused me to lift my head from the pillow and look across my body, directly into Papa's face. At that instant, I saw his face bathed in tears and I heard him cry out, "Dear God, Oral is our baby boy and he's going to die and he doesn't seem to realize it! He's paid no attention to You! O God, save him . . . PLEASE!"

> **IN A FLASH OF DIVINE INSPIRATION, I LOOKED UP AS PAPA'S FACE FADED AND IN ITS PLACE I SAW THE IMAGE OF JESUS!**

My soul erupted! My belly rolled over and the pressure rushed up to my tongue. It felt like my inner being burst wide open and I began to bawl like a baby. I heard myself calling, "O God, save my soul! Jesus, save me!"

I'll tell you, at that instant, no one had to tell

Oral Roberts how to pray because, when I saw the image of Jesus' face, it broke my heart up, and the Lord became all that I desired in the whole world!

In a moment's time, I felt the presence of God come rushing into my head and surge through my body until I felt as light as a feather. When I glanced around the room, I blinked my eyes because it was like someone had flipped the lights on — I mean, brilliant lights. It was like I had escaped from a world of darkness into a world of light!

I FELT MY BELLY AREA COME ALIVE AS WORDS BEGAN TO RISE UP IN ME

From the deepest reaches of my belly area words began to pour out over my tongue as tears gushed from my eyes, "God, I repent that I've ignored You. I'm sorry! Jesus, I give You my life! What little I've got left, I give it! I give it! I give it!"

Quick as lightning, from my innermost being, I felt a warming. Then a force shot through me like an electrical current, racing through my body, over and over again. No one had to tell Oral Roberts he was saved. I knew I had been soundly converted, made a new creature in Christ, a newborn Christian. What Papa and Mamma had not been able to convince me to do even once in those five months, a fleeting glimpse of the face of Jesus Christ had caused me to do in one split second!

As everyone rushed around me, rejoicing, we all began to weep and laugh and praise God and, suddenly, something strange happened. Immediately upon receiving Christ as my Lord and Savior, I felt an electrifying awareness that God was in the room with me, and I had a tremendous "welling-up" feeling in the pit of my stomach. <u>My belly area came alive, and there was the strangest sensation that words were coming up in me.</u> Not English words, but words of another language — words I'd never heard before.

I had heard of the baptism with the Holy Spirit, and my parents had testified they had received this marvelous experience from the Lord. On occasion I had heard, as had my brothers and sister, unusual words pour forth from their lips as they prayed or praised God "in the Spirit." They called it "speaking with tongues," according to Acts 2:4, and they said it made them feel a tremendous warmth and a peace in their belly area, what they assumed was their inner man. But beyond that, they knew and said very little about it. You see, Papa had been reared a Methodist and Mamma was a Missionary Baptist and not much light was shed upon the Holy Spirit through their denominational upbringing.

I know it had never captured my attention, not because it wasn't a reality to them or of benefit, but it was like scores of other things about God to which I was exposed in my childhood: I had chosen to ignore it and I simply gave it no thought. I knew I had dear and beloved parents and we were a closely knit family, but that's as far as my thoughts went, including my thoughts concerning "tongues."

Now my point here is a very important one. Had I known then what I came to know years later when I had reached the point of girdling the globe with the Gospel and building God a university, *I could have spoken in tongues the very instant after Christ came into my life!* (See Acts 10:25-48.)

I mean, the Spirit of God was rolling around in my belly like a mighty river flowing, and I felt so good inside I thought I would burst! <u>The movement was upward and into my mouth, and my tongue was instantly engaged to speak words I had never learned before.</u> My entire being felt like it was virtually consumed with the sheer force of this mighty river, but either surprise or a fear of the unknown struck me and I desisted.

How did I desist? I simply chose not to let those words that were rolling up in me pour forth out of my mouth, and in a few moments that powerful, extraordinary force subsided. Of course, I was gloriously saved, rejoicing with my parents at my newfound salvation through Jesus Christ (although I was still terminally ill, bedfast with the tuberculosis).

But, oh, what one doesn't know is often so

costly! All the years of the first half of my healing ministry could have been daily interlaced and miraculously energized by a talking God and a talking man conversing in a "language of the Spirit." This would have opened up my inner man to the deeper things of God sooner, and it would have benefited me immensely in the struggles of my life . . . especially when I was under the indescribable pressures of attempting to get God's university underway.

The fact is, it wasn't I who was waiting for God. He was waiting for me to "listen up," to catch up to the fact that He is not a silent God, but a God Who is so tender and responsive that we humans have yet to grasp just how close He is to each of us. We have failed to realize that we can talk to Him as naturally as breathing and ***WE CAN HEAR HIM TALK TO US JUST AS EASILY!***

And while we can do this to a certain extent by what the Church calls "walking with God," we can talk to Him in a far greater and more understandable way by "talking" to Him through "tongues," and then stopping and listening for Him to speak to us as we "interpret" back to our minds what He is saying.

I know I have been visited by the Lord in a most marvelous way through this kind of a "talking" relationship with our Heavenly Father!

Does this sound far out? It certainly did to me.

When those first few syllables came rushing up inside me only moments after I had received Christ as my personal Lord and Savior, I didn't understand it and I chose to stop it, and I robbed myself of one of the sweetest experiences of my life!

I can only state sincerely and honestly that when the day came that I yielded to this glorious and marvelous and deep-moving experience by "releasing" what I had learned to call "my prayer and praise language of the Holy Spirit," there was an illumination of God and of things of a higher spiritual dimension which suddenly began to open within me. It was only then that I could be the person and do the things for the Lord which I had only partially dreamed of and meditated on, and which I had never before thought possible!

> **REALLY, IT'S THE MOST EXQUISITE AND SOUL-SATISFYING EXPERIENCE THAT I (AND MILLIONS OF OTHER DEVOTED CHRISTIANS) HAVE DAILY WITH THE LORD!**

Oh, friend, this experience is real! It isn't a cure-all, but it is wonderful beyond words and it can help you find God's miracle answers to your needs! And I have so much more to share with you about this fantastic experience of talking to God in tongues and, by interpretation, hearing Him talk back to you (which continues the explicit release of your prayer and praise language as a child of God). ***It still fascinates me and is the cream of my walk with God!***

Chapter 3

"ORAL, CAN I HEAR THE VOICE OF GOD?"

It was a brilliant, beautiful Saturday morning as the sun streaked across the fairway at Southern Hills Country Club in Tulsa, Oklahoma. I was standing there talking with my foursome and hitting a few practice shots as we prepared to tee off. To get to play an entire game is a rare treat for me because, with my pressing schedule in the ministry, I usually only have time to run out and play a few holes whenever I can.

Actually, because of the call of God on my life, I had never even attempted to play golf until I was 35 years old. And, in spite of the fact that I did not have the opportunity to play regularly, I was still a pretty good striker of the ball!

At this particular time I was in my late 40s, just beginning my tenure as founding president of Oral Roberts University and, because Southern Hills had invited the president of the University of Tulsa, Dr. Eugene Swearingen, to join their country club, they graciously extended the same invitation to me

as founder/president of ORU. Otherwise, I probably never would have become a member of Tulsa's
most prestigious country club.

This strikingly beautiful golf course is located
only one mile from the ORU campus, so it was
handy for me to run by after a full day's work and
play a few holes or a whole game or simply to
practice. I had managed to achieve a six handicap
and, of the 600 golfing members in the club, I was
one of only 25 who had accomplished that. It was
precisely for this reason that certain people became
interested in my ministry. They admired a good
low-handicap golfer who was not a professional.

In that background and that setting on a
beautiful sun-drenched Oklahoma morning, a doctor, a great heart specialist, walked up to our
foursome and tapped me on the shoulder.

"Oral," he asked hesitantly, "have you got a
minute before you tee off?"

"Sure," I replied quickly.

Walking over to a spot where we could talk
more privately, I noticed that he looked troubled,
almost like he was ready to burst into tears, and his
lip was trembling. "Is there something wrong, Bill?"
I asked.

"Oral, I'm a doctor and you're a preacher and
you're the one man I know in Tulsa who can help
me!"

"I'll sure try," I assured him.

"Well, God has blessed me in my medical practice, I've felt His hand on my life many times, but I've never heard His voice . . . never heard Him speak to me." His eyes welled up. I waited.

"You're the one man I feel comfortable in asking a question that's been troubling me."

"What is it, Bill?" I pondered.

He dropped his head, looked up and then, with his eyes fastened on mine, he asked, "CAN I HEAR THE VOICE OF GOD?"

Without hesitation I exclaimed, "Of course you can! Everybody can hear God's voice."

"But, Oral, I mean ME! Can I hear Him speak to ME personally? I know you're a man of God; you're supposed to hear His voice. But I'm a layman. I don't know the Bible like you do. I spend my time operating on people, and there are times that if I could somehow hear God speak to me, even in just a whisper, maybe I could save a whole lot more lives!"

"Stay right here," I told him. "I'll be back."

I went over to my foursome and asked them to go ahead, and I told them I would join them in a few holes. Then, returning to my doctor friend, I said, "Let's go over here and sit down and talk and wait on God."

After we found a secluded spot to resume our conversation, I asked him, "Bill, you talk TO God, don't you?"

"I try," he replied quietly.

"I mean, you do speak to Him out of your spirit, even saying words to Him?" I asked.

"Yes, quite often. But I've never actually heard Him speak back to me," he murmured, shaking his head.

"Okay. Let's consider for a moment the fact that as a person you have the ability to talk; in other words, *you are a talking person.*" He nodded. "In the same way would you say *God is a talking God*?" I asked.

"Ah, yes, I've always believed that. As a Christian, how could I not believe it? Also, I've heard you say you've heard God's voice. I once heard you declare that everyone can hear His voice. But if I have, I wasn't aware He was speaking to me! I really want to know how to hear the voice of the Lord."

"Now, let me say something to you which I believe the Bible fully supports and which I have personally experienced and have seen others experience in the most practical and intelligent way when they get serious enough with God."

"I sure want to hear it," he sighed.

"Bill, have you ever spoken in tongues as the Holy Spirit gives you utterance?" I asked.

"No," he replied, "but I've read about it in the Bible and I understand that you do."

"I not only speak in tongues by the Spirit," I told him, "but I also pray to interpret what God is saying

37

back to me. This is what the Apostle Paul tells us to do in I Corinthians 14:13, 'Wherefore let him that speaketh in an unknown tongue pray that he may interpret.' I'm not saying that Paul is necessarily saying that every time we pray or praise in tongues, we are to follow it by praying that He will enable us to interpret.

"But if we can grasp what the Apostle is saying, tongues are not only to edify (or strengthen our spirit, our inner man), but they are to lead us to ask God to speak back to us -- either telling us in our own language what we SAID to Him in tongues or telling us His RESPONSE to what we said to Him in tongues.

"The fact that God says if we pray in tongues we are to pray for God to interpret back to us what we said, or His response to what we said, means to me that when we pray in tongues, we should condition our spirit to ask God to speak back to us through interpretation.

"Remember, interpretation is not translation, God doesn't translate what we spoke in tongues, or His response to it. He <u>interprets</u> the meaning which we really need to <u>hear and know</u>."

Bill said, "If I should be filled with the Holy Spirit and begin the practice of speaking in tongues, are you saying I can expect the interpretation to come back from God each time?"

"No, I don't know that He will give His answer

38

by interpretation each time. I do know that I seldom pray in tongues without asking for the interpretation. Sometimes I'm blessed simply by praying in tongues and letting it edify my spirit. However, I believe God said to pray for the interpretation so we can hear Him speak back to our minds."

"Oral, this is pretty deep for me, but I may be catching on. Are you saying that if I pray in tongues, I am talking TO God, and if I follow that by praying to Him for the interpretation, He is actually speaking back to me -- and I can hear Him speak TO me?"

"I'm saying exactly that. Interpretation is not the only way God speaks to you. He speaks through His Word, through your hearing His Word preached, through His speaking directly into your spirit, even audibly at times, and in other ways as well. However, God is sovereign; that is, He can do what He wants to do. But speaking TO God in tongues and praying for Him to speak back the interpretation TO us is a way that I believe each Holy Spirit-filled believer can experience Him speaking to them. Of course, what we hear by interpretation must be in harmony with the Word of God."

"Oral, how does the interpretation come? How can I know it is God's interpretation back to me, that it is God speaking to me and not just my imagining it?"

"My personal experience, and that of others I know that do it, is this: when I finish praying in tongues -- a few seconds or minutes -- I pray for interpretation. That's right, I ask God for it just as the Apostle Paul says in I Corinthians 14:13.

"Then I pause, get quiet, and listen. I'm waiting on God to speak back to my mind to give me <u>understanding</u> of the tongues which, Paul says, is 'a mystery' (I Corinthians 14:2). I don't understand a thing I say in tongues; it bypasses my mind and goes straight to God. Therefore, in asking for interpretation I'm asking God to reveal the mystery, to open it up to my <u>understanding</u>, which is to my mind, my intellect. I can always get edified by tongues alone, but I can't get understanding back in my mind unless God answers my prayer for the interpretation."

"Oral, can you make that a little more personal?"

"I'll try. For me, when I'm waiting on the interpretation and I'm listening with my spirit, sometimes nothing -- not a word -- comes back at that moment. At other times, I'm able to see the words as if they were written on a page and which I can say out loud to myself. Then, at times, God's full response comes and my mind receives it. I begin to say it and I feel my mind being illuminated, like a light is turned on, and I hear God saying specific things to me concerning my life, or about doing certain things, or telling me just to rest in Him.

"Bill, when it comes in my mind like this, my

understanding is increased greatly. It seems in that instance that my mind is sharper and I am able to grasp spiritual things much better than before I prayed in tongues and received God's interpretation back."

"Oral, do you get this every time?"

"I can't say I do every time. Here's where faith comes in. As I speak in tongues, then follow it by praying for the interpretation, I must believe that God is a talking God, as I am a talking person, and that by tongues I have initiated a conversation with Him, and eventually -- if I focus my spirit on Him -- I am sure I will get the interpretation. If not at that moment, then perhaps later that day or a week or two later. It's uncanny how you can learn to know and recognize it is an interpretation from the Lord. You've just got to get into it with your spirit totally open to God, hungry to hear Him speak to you, and start believing that He will. It is an act of your faith to speak to God in tongues, also an act of your faith to receive His interpretation."

Bill said, "Can you give me an example of what you've heard back by interpretation?"

"Yes, I can. When Evelyn and I received the news of the tragic death in a plane crash of our daughter, Rebecca, and her husband, Marshall Nash, we had to go to their house and tell their three little children that their mommy and daddy weren't coming home. We were so devastated we couldn't pray very well. Instantly, through our tears, Evelyn and I began praying in tongues. Halfway through, I paused and waited for the interpretation. Very clearly I heard, 'God knows something about this that we don't know.'

"Immediately I told Evelyn this interpretation. It had the most calming effect upon us. It helped us know God was still in control and we could depend on Him in a situation that had torn us up and confused our minds. By the time we arrived at the house to talk to our three little grandchildren, now orphans, we were in possession of ourselves, and that really helped those little ones as nothing else could."

Bill said, "My wife and I were praying for you as soon as we heard the news. You may remember, the media picked up on what you said God had told you -- that He knew something about this that you didn't know."

"The media carried that statement all over the world," I told him. "I received much mail concerning it and how it helped explain something that had been beyond understanding. That leads me to share a further word about the value God puts on understanding."

"I'd like to hear it," Bill said.

Taking my little New Testament out of my pocket, I turned to I Corinthians 14:13-15 where Paul says, "Wherefore let him that speaketh in an unknown tongue pray that he may interpret. For if I pray in an unknown tongue, my spirit prayeth, but my understanding is unfruitful. What is it then? I will pray with the spirit, and I will pray with the understanding also: I will sing with the spirit, and I will sing with the understanding also."

"First, look where Paul said that if you pray in tongues, pray that you may interpret. Second, look where Paul explains this in terms of how the interpretation speaks to your understanding or to your mind. He says when he prayed in the Spirit (tongues), his mind was unfruitful; that is, his mind did not understand the mystery of what he was saying to God in tongues. He said it was his spirit praying (not his mind). Then he asks what should he do at that time. He answers by saying, 'I will pray with the spirit, AND I will pray WITH THE UNDERSTANDING ALSO.'"

Bill said, "What does he mean when he says he will pray both in tongues and with his understanding, also?"

I replied, "First, I think he is saying that praying in tongues is subject to our will. In other words, we will to pray in tongues. It is not under the control of our emotions, but our will, making it a prayer with order, and not just emotionalism. Next, I think he is explaining that he doesn't stop when he finishes praying in the Spirit (tongues), but he prays for the interpretation -- and when he gets it, it becomes UNDERSTANDING to him that he didn't have before. And then he prays in that understanding. It is like when God said He knew something about Rebecca and Marshall's deaths that we didn't know, and an understanding came to our minds that we were not left alone with this tragedy in our family. With that understanding illuminating and enlightening our minds, we were able both to pray and act out of that Holy Spirit-inspired understanding which I had received by interpretation."

Bill said, "Then you actually heard God speak to you in those words that He knew something about it you did not know?"

I said, "Yes, I heard the words distinctly. I remember my friend, Bob Schuller, pastor of the Crystal Cathedral and a TV minister, being quoted by the media about what those words meant to him. He actually quoted them over his Sunday morning service on television."

Bill wanted to talk some more. I forgot about my golf game and stayed with him until he was through. "Is there some interpretation you've received on an everyday matter or concern?"

One came to me. I said, "Well, I was behind schedule recently and was rushing around and upsetting everybody. I just couldn't get control of things, and I was not really myself. Suddenly, I willed to pray in tongues, since my prayers through my mind were not helping me. I stopped dead still and listened for the interpretation. Sure enough, here it came: 'Slow down, sit down, get your mind on your Source, and let Me adjust your schedule.'"

Bill said, "Did God say that?"

I replied, "Yes."

"What did you do?" he asked.

I answered, "At the exact time the interpretation got into my understanding, I slowed down. I found a chair and sat down, and I willed my mind off my problem and onto looking to God as my Source of total supply, which is the first of the three keys to the MIRACLE OF SEED-FAITH."

"Did it work?"

"It did. I simmered down, took a load off my mind, got to thinking about the Lord, Who I knew had faced rougher schedules than mine, and finally got control of myself. Almost before I knew it, things began falling into place. The day was over and I had forgotten about how I had been running around like a chicken with its head cut off. I actually had a good day!"

"And you believe God spoke to you through that?"

"I know He did."

"Oral, do you know the thing that this is clearing up the most for me? I'm learning that I don't have to hear God's audible voice when He speaks to me. I see that there are so many other ways He also uses to speak, like through interpretation. But I still want you to write that little book for me."

We shook hands and had a little prayer together, and I caught my golf foursome on the second nine holes.

As I returned to my group, I realized anew how much more simple -- and desirable -- the Apostle Paul makes speaking in tongues and praying for the interpretation. When receiving it back from God in His own words, it enters our understanding so THAT WE CAN PRAY WITH UNDERSTANDING, RATHER THAN PRAY THE PROBLEM.

Thinking back on my conversation with Bill, the heart surgeon whose concern to hear God speak to him was so deep, I know more than ever how enormously important the prayer language of the Spirit is. <u>All believers can use it in their daily prayer life and hear God speak back to them</u>. Maybe not every time. Also, not as easily or commonly at first, but we hear better and better the more we use our will.

I cannot say it often enough -- you have to <u>will</u> to do it. Paul said, "I will," and it must be the same with using our will. Not wishing, not hoping that somehow it will be like being struck by lightning, but willing it, looking for it, expecting it, and using it on a daily basis.

I've been asked how often I pray in tongues. I answer, "Probably twenty or thirty times a day."

Why so many times?

Because I have great needs. I need supernatural help, and I am desiring more and more the very practical and valuable experience of praying in tongues.

As I've already indicated, in using my prayer language daily I sometimes do it to edify myself only, and not to interpret. However, I wish to emphasize that I believe the higher purpose of tongues beyond edifying oneself is to make our mind (intellect) gain a deeper understanding of how to better serve God -- better live our lives on a more practical Christian basis -- and to continually desire our talking God to talk to us, His talking children. Through interpretation, I believe -- and constantly experience -- that He talks back to me in words that increase my understanding.

God said, "With all thy getting get understanding" (Proverbs 4:7). This is a powerful New Testament way to do it.

I've also been asked if I receive an <u>answer</u> to every prayer I pray by using both my prayer language and praying by my spirit through my mind without tongues.

I can honestly say, no, not visibly. While I believe God answers every sincere prayer, when prayed according to His Will, the answers aren't always immediately forthcoming or visible to our senses, although many, many times they are.

God will answer our prayers. There may be some answers we'll not see in this lifetime, but when we enter eternity and look back, I believe we'll see that no answer to prayer failed.

Of course, prayer is meant mostly to help us in this life -- to bring us to a saving knowledge of the Lord Jesus, to healings, miracles, God's presence, His guidance, to helping win souls, spreading the Gospel, and daily finding help in every area of our lives. So answers to prayer are to come to us in this life; however, it's my conviction we will never see all the answers until we enter God's own presence when we die and go to Heaven.

When the Holy Spirit is as helpful in our prayers as Jesus says He is, the Lord sends Him as another Comforter, the Paraclete, meaning "One called alongside to help." Not only is He "in" us, abiding with us forever, but He "helps" us. In my understanding of the Word and my experience, the prayer language -- with the ever present possibility of receiving interpretation back to our mind to our understanding -- is something I can't afford to do without. And I urge every believer to grasp this reality for themselves.

PRAYING IN THE SPIRIT
WITH THE INTERPRETATION
CAN RELEASE THE MIRACULOUS
IN YOUR LIFE

It has taken me far longer than I had hoped to write the book I promised my friend, the heart specialist, that I would write, but I'm glad I wrote it. The Spirit prompted me to go all the way back to Jesus and the first Christians in the first century, and to illustrate in the simplest of terms the value of this great experience of SPEAKING IN TONGUES WITH THE INTERPRETATION. Not only so I could understand and practice this Bible way of praying much better for myself, but so that those who know little or nothing about it from a scriptural stand-point could catch a glimpse of what's in it for them, personally. I especially wanted them to see how it could enable them to speak TO GOD in an even deeper dimension and have God speak TO THEM, ***thus releasing the power of the miraculous in their lives!***

Now I want to make it clear that the very first time I heard God speaking directly to me, I knew almost nothing of SPEAKING IN TONGUES WITH THE INTERPRETATION. In fact, I knew little or nothing about God speaking to a person at all, and I most certainly was not expecting Him to speak to me!

But the Lord did whisper His words in my heart while I was on my way to be prayed for by a healing evangelist the very night I was healed from tubercu-losis in the final stages . . . and God has spoken to me in different ways some 22 times since that night.

Each time, major events have evolved out of hearing Him speak to me.

That's one way God speaks -- when one is not expecting it. At other times, He speaks when a person is earnestly desiring and seeking to hear God's voice. However, that's not what I'm talking about when I use the term SPEAKING IN TONGUES WITH THE INTERPRETATION, which is a result of having been baptized with the Holy Spirit. This is an experience which I have been led to call THE PRAYER LANGUAGE OF THE SPIRIT, which is easier for most people to grasp, I think.

You need to pray out of your spirit, because there are times when your mind simply doesn't know how to express to the Lord what you're feeling deep inside in your spirit man.

Receiving the INTERPRETATION back is literally God speaking directly TO YOU. His words may come to you in the form of "a word of knowledge" from above, or "a word of wisdom," or "a word of discernment" (I Corinthians 12). Or the interpretation may come in other ways in which something is said TO YOUR MIND or through an impression deep in your spirit. And, of course, every revelation from the Lord *WILL AGREE WITH THE WORD OF GOD* and never depart from its principles nor add to it, because the Bible says the Spirit and the Word agree. (See I John 5:7.)

> **WHAT THE PRAYER LANGUAGE OF THE SPIRIT REALLY IS, IS YOUR SPIRIT BYPASSING YOUR MIND (INTELLECT) *MOMENTARILY* AS YOU, BY YOUR WILL, SPEAK TO GOD IN WAYS YOUR MIND CANNOT.**

I believe this marvelous process will become more real to you if you'll look for a moment at the little drawings I made back in the early '60s as one of the first leaders of the Charismatic movement. This movement has become a beautiful, powerful and useful dimension of the classical Pentecostal movement out of which I was gloriously saved and healed and called to take God's healing power to my generation.

The best way I know of to describe it is the *Pentecostal/Charismatic* movement. Oh, how I love them both! The Pentecostal movement is the base, the underpinning, while the Charismatic movement embraces a greater and more frequent release of the gifts of the Spirit. (See I Corinthians 12.) I believe that together they have the most penetrating revelation of the Scriptures by the Holy Spirit that I have ever known and continue to experience! (See drawings on page 54.)

UNDERSTANDING ON THE HIGHEST LEVEL
OF THE GOD/MAN EXISTENCE

Perhaps the most important word to us as
human beings, the word that marks the bottom line
of our lives, is the word UNDERSTANDING. Having
understanding draws us closer to God and to each
other and produces "unity in the Spirit." Not having
understanding separates us from the Lord, isolates
us from each other and spawns divisions among us.
This leads to wars, to the splitting apart of our
homes, to the disintegration of our personal lives,
and to the shattering of peace in every area of our
existence.

What my doctor friend was hungering for when
he asked me to help him hear God speak to him was
to **understand** on the highest level of the God/man
existence. He wanted to be a better Christian, a
better doctor, a better human being, a better con-
tributor of his gifts and his life to hurting, suffering
humanity, and to be able to go beyond the limits of
his human selfhood all the way to that realm where
he and God are one . . . united, caring, loving,
creating, and having the "good success" that the
Bible speaks about. (See Joshua 1:8.)

And that's exactly why I'm writing this book —
to help my friend Bill and myself and every child of
God to bridge the gulf between our own limited
human knowledge and the God Who possesses all

knowledge and understanding . . . so the problem of not knowing, not understanding, is suddenly ANSWERED!

You see, when we *pray in the Spirit with the understanding and then get the interpretation back*, the Holy Spirit illuminates our minds, enabling us to grasp the knowledge we need, as He reveals to us the will and purpose of God in this earth. He opens our minds and causes them to blossom until suddenly we can conceive of ideas like God does, think like God thinks, and **the Holy Spirit begins to unlock for us the realm of the miraculous that we're longing with all of our hearts to enter!**

Now let me describe how this experience of the Holy Spirit burst onto the scene of the modern-day Church, and how it can happen in your life and the lives of your loved ones.

1.
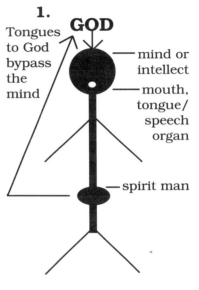

Tongues
to God
bypass
the
mind

GOD

— mind or intellect

— mouth, tongue/ speech organ

— spirit man

Tongues

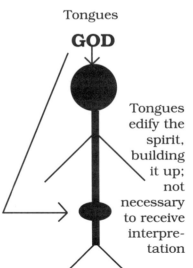

GOD

Tongues edify the spirit, building it up; not necessary to receive interpretation

2.
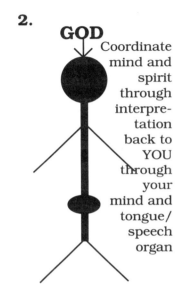

GOD

Coordinate mind and spirit through interpretation back to YOU through your mind and tongue/ speech organ

Tongues and Interpretation

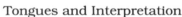
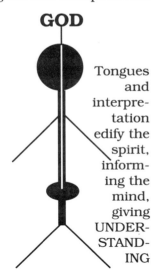

GOD

Tongues and interpretation edify the spirit, informing the mind, giving UNDERSTANDING

54

SPEAKING WITH TONGUES AND WITH THE UNDERSTANDING -- THE CHRISTIAN'S ENTRY INTO THE MIRACULOUS

There are those in the Body of Christ today who believe that God ceased speaking to man centuries ago, that there are no longer any visions or revelations, that the beachhead was established and the Church was birthed into this world and now we are simply keepers of the flame and not extenders of the vision. They believe this powerful experience of *speaking with tongues with the understanding* died out when the last of the original apostles died.

But I submit to you that this experience of the Holy Ghost and fire **IS** the experience of power, of boldness, of the glory and presence of God upon which Jesus Christ Himself founded the Christian Church. And it was through this experience that the disciples in the first century were able to au-thenticate the Christian faith . . . to work great miracles of deliverance, to bring healing to the people, and to cause multiplied thousands of lost souls to come streaming into the kingdom of God!

I will not take issue with the philosophy and theology of those who believe that tongues are "not for today." But I will gladly testify to the validity of this marvelous experience of the Holy Spirit's power in my own life! <u>And I'm not ashamed to declare that I believe speaking with tongues is absolutely necessary for a thrilling Christian life in today's world!</u> Because *speaking with tongues with the interpretation* is the Christian's ENTRY INTO THE REALM OF THE MIRACULOUS! That's why those of us who believe in it and practice it **EXPECT AND BELIEVE GREATER THINGS LIE AHEAD FOR THE BODY OF CHRIST TODAY!** And that's what I want to see happen in your life, too — GREATER THINGS!

MY PARENTS HAD A GLIMPSE
OF THE MIRACULOUS NATURE
OF THE CHRISTIAN LIFE

I praise God for parents who had at least a partial understanding of the miraculous way the Christian experience is supposed to operate in the life of a newborn Christian. As I lay there on the bed of affliction, hemorrhaging to death with a terminal illness, they led me to receive Jesus Christ as my personal Lord and Savior. And at that moment the

Lord became more real to me than any human being on the face of the earth.

I actually felt His presence rushing through my body. Oh, friend, don't let anyone kid you to believe that you cannot feel the presence of God. <u>Let me tell you, when He Who built this world gets inside a little thing like you or me, you can feel Him moving in your soul!</u>

That very first instant when God came into my life, I felt miraculous power surging through my body, and it lifted me and I was able to stand on my feet. You see, during the five months I was bedfast, I had lost the strength to walk. But all at once as God's Spirit flooded up in me that night, I was able to get up out of the bed and dance around that little room with my mother and father, shouting and praising God! I knew I was soundly converted. The Lord Jesus Christ had supernaturally transformed my sinful nature and filled my soul with the light and life of God and I had an insatiable desire to serve the Lord forever!

THE HOLY GHOST EVANGELISTS
OPENED THE REALM OF THE MIRACULOUS
TO ORDINARY PEOPLE

I'll never forget all the stories Mamma and Papa told us children about the Holy Spirit-filled evangelists who came into Pontotoc County, Oklahoma, where I was born and raised. Immediately upon hearing these men full of the Spirit preach and sing the old-fashioned gospel songs, my father, a Methodist, and my mother, a Baptist, received the baptism with the Holy Spirit with the initial evidence of speaking in tongues. That is, the first sign that they were filled or baptized with the Holy Spirit was the fact that they began to speak in tongues according to Acts 2:4.

In those days, when the Holy Ghost evangelists crossed the southwest frontier with their full-gospel message, it was really like plowing up brand-new ground. People who had studied the Bible sufficiently to understand that every Christian believer could receive the fullness of the Holy Spirit's power were few and far between.

When they did receive, they spoke with tongues and felt the miraculous touch of God in their souls in the form of an inner therapy, an edifying of their spirits, and an overwhelming urge or feeling that ***they could have all God had for them!*** Almost subconsciously at first, they grasped that they could believe for miracles of healing, miracle interventions in their daily lives. Really, they believed God would move Heaven and earth in their behalf! ***IT WAS AN ENTRY INTO THE MIRACULOUS!***

The little churches that had sprung up all across the frontier were composed primarily of people who had not been taught about the Holy

Spirit and subsequently did not receive the light on it. As a result, when the Holy Ghost evangelists sent their revival fires streaking across the prairies, it was mostly outside the organized denominational churches.

It was the unchurched, the sinners, the sick, the hungry and the poverty-stricken who saw God in a different light. They had seen nothing miraculous in any of the churches they knew about, other than receiving Christ as their personal Savior. Miracles of healing and other manifestations of the supernatural that could touch their physical and material lives were missing from many of the organized churches. Of course, they had seen the supernatural *in the spiritual realm* — the salvation of the soul — but the spiritual was still difficult to comprehend.

Many of the unchurched who responded to the Holy Ghost evangelists were like my parents. Papa and Mamma were listed as members on a church roll but they were not born again, and definitely not attendants on Sunday, the Church not being a vital part of their lives.

My parents were sharecroppers with three young children at that time (later there were five, one of which died with pneumonia) and they were just barely subsisting rather than living. To them, going to church services consisted of hearing the choir sing the beautiful old hymns and a pastor preach a sermon, with an invitation to join the church which included a heavily disguised part about believing on Jesus for a supernatural salvation. But to them God seemed to be somewhere way up in the Milky Way, so distant and unreal. Their hearts were hungry for something more, something that gave them hope in dealing with the bare realities of living and in overcoming the harshness of their sharecropper existence. That same reason remains true for people today. We must have the MIRACULOUS <u>in order to deal with the realities of our lives.</u>

The Holy Ghost evangelists were a different breed of Christian. They were full of vitality and enthusiasm for the Lord as they sang, preached, and invited people to turn their lives over to God and enter the Church of Jesus Christ. When they sang, it was with the joy of the Lord bursting from their hearts and the glory shining on their faces. They preached like men and women on fire, with their whole beings thrown into their sermons, and wonderful, miraculous power poured from their souls into everyone who listened.

They preached that to be saved by the blood of Jesus on the cross was a supernatural AND TOTAL change of your heart and life, that you would "feel" the power of God through and through and that, when you were converted, it happened in the flash of a second, it was instantaneous, and you would know it! ***You would be a new creation, vibrant and alive in God!***

There was shouting, dancing "in the Spirit" and falling "under the power." Sick people suddenly felt a surge of new hope, people with troublesome habits saw they could be freed, and those who were down and out saw themselves rising up into God's abundant life!

Next, the Holy Ghost evangelists preached the Bible texts that had long been neglected: texts on the baptism with the Holy Ghost which taught that as a believer you received the gift of the Holy Spirit and could instantly speak in tongues. They declared that the apostles had received the initial outpouring of the Holy Ghost on the day of Pentecost and the early Christians had received the outpouring of the Spirit in the Samaritan revival, the Ephesian revival, the Caesarean revival, the outpouring in the house of Cornelius, and the great baptism with the Holy Ghost that Paul, the apostle, received after being touched by the Lord on the road to Damascus.

They also proclaimed, as Peter had done on the day of Pentecost, that **WHOSOEVER WILL** could receive this Holy Ghost power as a vital, living force in their lives! (See Acts 2:39.) In other words, they believed and taught that every man, woman, boy and girl could have a direct pipeline to the Almighty! ***They opened the realm of the miraculous to***

ordinary people. And many were like my parents
. . . eager to cast their lot with a group of believers
who were not intimidated by the world's onslaughts,
but who exalted the living God and ***REFUSED TO
DENY HIS HOLY GHOST POWER!***

And before you're through reading this book, I
believe you're going to desire that same power in
your own life if you've never experienced it, and in
a greater way if you have it already.

Chapter 5

THE HOLY SPIRIT: THE UNLIMITED PRESENCE OF JESUS IN THE EARTH

Jesus Christ came down to earth because something was terribly wrong with the world. It was a world of spiritual and moral darkness, a world of suffering, a world of brutality and crime. When He came into the world, into the midst of mortal men, He challenged the satanic intruders and cast them out. The Bible proclaims, "For this purpose the Son of God was manifested, THAT HE MIGHT DESTROY THE WORKS OF THE DEVIL" (I John 3:8)! The Son of God came down to earth with His sword of faith dipped in the blood of Calvary, and His mission from His Father was to deliver mankind from the devil's cruel grip!

It appears that the world into which Jesus came was filled with a multitude of satanic intruders, that evil forces had combined in their purposes against God and against the human beings He had created. And Christ, in answer to the screaming, tormenting needs of humanity, was sent of God to drive out the evil forces and **SET MAN FREE!**

Yes, it was a great time in this earth when Jesus walked the dusty roads of Judea and the cobblestone streets of Jerusalem, stretching out His hands to heal the sick and release the captives from their deadly bonds. He was a solitary figure, spaced in time and eternity, walking among men as the mighty Savior, the triumphant Master, as the Son of God and Son of Man.

He called strong men to His side to be His disciples, sending them forth into this sin-cursed earth to heal the sick, to raise the dead and cast out devils. And the Bible says they returned with great joy, declaring, "Lord, even the devils are subject unto us through thy name" (Luke 10:17). They could do those mighty works because He said for them to do so, and because, with their very own eyes, THEY HAD SEEN HIM DO THE WONDERFUL WORKS OF GOD!

On the last night of the Lord's earthly life, the disciples were suddenly struck with terror when He announced to them that He was withdrawing His physical presence from them. Anticipating their fears, He said, "Verily, verily," or truly, truly, "I say unto you, He that believeth on me, the works that I do shall he do also; and **greater works than these shall he do; BECAUSE I GO UNTO MY FATHER**" (John 14:12).

How could this be? the disciples must have

wondered, as they shuddered at the very thought of the Master leaving their sides. Jesus gave them the key when He said, "I will send you another Comforter and He will be with you forever." (See John 14:16.) He was telling them, "Another member of the divine Godhead will come and take My place among you — the Holy Spirit."

IN OTHER WORDS, JESUS WAS SAYING, "THERE IS TO BE *NO INTERRUPTION* OF THE MIGHTY WORKS OF GOD IN THIS EARTH!"

His words jolted them, but the reality of what He was saying just didn't sink in. They couldn't imagine that He, as they had seen Him with their eyes and touched Him with their hands, was going to ascend into Heaven and they would no longer be with Him in the flesh. Oh, my! They had built their entire lives around Him!

When the Man of Galilee walked up to them and cried, "Follow Me," in those two little words they felt the measure of time and eternity and they sensed the power of the Lord drawing them to His side. "Follow Me," Jesus said, and strong men left their trades, their businesses, gave up everything and followed a total stranger, a man they had never seen before!

But now He was telling them, "I must go away." Can you imagine the thoughts that must have flooded their minds, the fears that must have ripped through their hearts? What if Christ had spent three years at your house in the flesh and then suddenly, without warning, He told you, "I must go away forever"? How would you feel? Abandoned and forlorn? Well, that's exactly how the disciples felt!

<u>Aren't there times when all of us feel so shaken up by something that we believe if we could only see Christ in the flesh, talk to Him face to face, hear a word from the lips of the Master, we would know how to tackle those problems that seem to be so unconquerable? We feel like we need the physical presence of Jesus right by our side!</u>

I remember how, as a young man, I had a dream that was bigger than myself and it seemed to be so terribly impossible. When I was only 29 1/2 years of age, attending a university and pastoring a small church in Enid, Oklahoma, the Lord began dealing with me about laying my hands upon people and praying for the healing of their sick, afflicted bodies. He was telling me that His time had come for me to take His healing power to my generation.

Now you must understand that back in 1947 when I first launched out into the ministry, healing was not understood like it is today. No one that I knew of was laying hands on the sick or praying for their healing, so it was up to people like me, who have the healing call of God on our lives, to pioneer a healing knowledge of the power of God in America and around the world.

But, in spite of all the obstacles, I still believed if I could somehow hear Christ's audible voice as I looked upon Him with my eyes (even as God had granted the Apostle Paul the opportunity to do) that I could go out and pray for the healing of the people as He had commanded me.

My heart was burning to pray for the sick, and I spent many intense hours alone with God, fasting, studying my Bible and crying out to Him in prayer. I remember one particular day when I reminded the Lord, "The people who lived in the days of Jesus were able to see Him with their natural eyes and talk with Him face to face. If I could only do that! If I could only see Christ in the flesh and feel Him as they felt Him and hear words from His own lips, then I know I could go out and pray for the sick like the apostles did!"

I was really wrestling before the Lord and yet it seemed as if I was not getting through when, all at once, God spoke to me in my spirit and said, "Oral, do you have the Holy Spirit?"

"Yes," I replied.

Then He asked me what may have been the most important question He has ever asked me, and it's a question I've been trying to answer ever since that day — ***"Do you know what you have?"***

I shrugged my shoulders and replied that I was certain I did not.

He continued by saying, "<u>When you have the Holy Spirit, it's exactly the same as having Me in the flesh right by your side.</u> For all practical purposes it's as if I'm walking beside you twenty-four hours a day, seven days a week. Everything I was to My disciples 2,000 years ago, I am to you now *by My Spirit*." And, friend, ***those were the words that clinched my victory!***

When I settled that issue in Oral Roberts' mind, something brand-new took hold of my being! I felt so good in my soul, I felt God erupting inside me! I suddenly grasped that when I had the Holy Spirit I was as well off as if Jesus Himself were walking right beside me in His seamless robe! And when the full realization of that began to sink down into my spirit, I cried, "Lord, I believe I can do what You've commanded me to do!"

Now this revelation will have an even greater impact on you if you realize that when Jesus walked this earth, His physical presence was contained in only one human body, which meant He could only be in one place at one time. When He was in Nazareth, He could not be in Caesarea. When He was in Jerusalem, He could not be in Bethany or Capernaum or anywhere else.

If the Lord were living on this earth today in His fleshly body and He were in one of the great cities of this nation — Los Angeles or New York or Dallas — *He could be nowhere else at that exact moment.* The important point is this: if Jesus in His physical body were at your house, He couldn't be at my house, too. Oh, my goodness! Now that puts an entirely different light on it, and *it makes the presence of the Holy Spirit even more precious!*

In my estimation, the greatest trial Jesus Christ ever faced was not the three temptations in the wilderness. (See Matthew 4:1-11.) His most formidable challenge was to remain confined to the constraints of His physical human body and to limit Himself and His miraculous power. When He was outside that earthly body, His power was limitless. So the physical body of Jesus Christ was a tremendous hindrance to Him, and **when He sent the Holy Spirit that hindrance was removed FOREVER!**

THE HOLY SPIRIT'S DRIVING PURPOSE
IS TO BRING JESUS CHRIST DOWN
FROM HEAVEN TO US!

The Holy Spirit's driving purpose is to bring the Lord Jesus Christ back down out of Heaven to us, not in the flesh but *in the Spirit.* The Holy Spirit brings Jesus to our side so we can do great exploits

69

with Him <u>today</u> just like we could have done had we lived 2,000 years ago, walking by His side, hearing the swish of His garments and the sound of His footsteps on the dusty, cobblestone streets.

My flesh tingles when I think about how, in the counsels of eternity, God looked into the future and saw our generation on fire and full of the Holy Ghost, with His Son Jesus living in our hearts, using us as vessels to perform His mighty works and to reach more people with the Gospel in one single hour than it was humanly possible for the Lord to reach while He walked this earth in the flesh!

Friend, I don't know about you, but I can shout and I can rejoice when I think about the unlimited, unending power that's flowing down to us from the cross of Jesus Christ at Calvary! And that awesome Holy Ghost power can be released in your life and mine by *praying in the Spirit with the understanding!*

So let Holy Ghost power FLOW through the Church of Jesus Christ! Let the Spirit of God fill us as individuals and as the Body of Christ with boldness and set our souls on fire for God! My brother, my sister, you can be a part of this life of miracles, this supernatural life of the Spirit! All you have to do is open the door and invite the Holy Spirit in! And when you do, there's a MIRACLE that bursts within you! There's a miracle that lives and moves within your being . . . ***AND EVERY DAY OF***

YOUR LIFE CAN BE A MIRACULOUS VISITATION FROM GOD!

Let it be like a mighty river flowing in you!

Chapter 6

A MIGHTY RUSHING
WIND FROM HEAVEN

Nothing stirred. There was no movement. No one made a sound, not even a whisper. It was like the silence in Heaven that the Bible speaks of. Then, all at once, like a bolt of lightning, a roar split the silence. As the wind sweeps over the sands of the desert and as the oil gushes up out of the ground and rushes toward the sky, there was a mighty rushing sound that filled the air, like the sound of a rushing wind from Heaven.

In a moment's time, the Holy Spirit whipped through the Upper Room like the holy wind of God! All of a sudden, there were flashes of God's power streaking down to earth as divine energy — as the fire of Heaven itself — and this divine Holy Ghost power began flooding up within the disciples of Jesus who were gathered in the Upper Room on the day of Pentecost.

Now these were the very same men who had walked the dusty roads of Judea and the sun-warmed shores of the sea of Galilee at the Master's side. They were there when the great crowds had gathered around Him in the streets of Jerusalem, clamoring to hear His words, to receive His healing touch! But these were also the very ones who went to pieces when their Savior hung His head on the cross and died. They had gone into hiding, terrified of the Jews, terrified of the Roman soldiers!

But when the Holy Ghost was poured out on the day of Pentecost, *all the hiding was over! All the confusion and consternation were banished!* As the Spirit of God fell upon the 120 disciples of Jesus, they were all filled with the Holy Ghost and spoke with other tongues as the Spirit gave them utterance! (See Acts 2:1-4.)

The 120 left the Upper Room that day with supernatural power from on high that broke like a tidal wave over the whole earth, and a tremendous crowd was drawn together when they heard that mighty, earthshaking phenomenon. The Bible says they were speaking with tongues and magnifying God, and the onlookers were astonished when they heard these unlearned Galileans declaring praises to God *in their own native tongues!*

As the Apostle Peter stood before that great assembled multitude, he boldly proclaimed, "But this is that which was spoken by the prophet Joel; And it shall come to pass in the last days, saith God, I will pour out of my Spirit upon all flesh" (Acts 2:16,17). Then his voice thundered a cry that was

73

heard throughout the centuries, ***"This Jesus hath God raised up, whereof we all are witnesses. Therefore being by the right hand of God exalted, and having received of the Father the promise of the Holy Ghost, he hath shed forth this, WHICH YE NOW SEE AND HEAR"*** (Acts 2:32,33)!

OH, HOW WONDERFUL IT IS TO KNOW THAT THE POWER OF OUR GOD CAN BE SEEN AND HEARD AND FELT AND DEMONSTRATED THROUGH US, HIS CHILDREN!

As divine Holy Ghost power erupted in the city of Jerusalem that day, men's hearts were convicted. They were pricked in their consciences, and over 3,000 were stirred to receive Jesus Christ as their Lord and Savior! (See Acts 2:41.)

And, friend, if you had been in the streets of Jerusalem on the day of Pentecost, you would have seen the glory and the splendor and the excitement and the power of the Holy Ghost and fire. It would not have been something to alarm you or confuse you. You would have grasped that this was what the Lord had, this was what the apostles had, this was the power that ignited the early Church. And it was this great and glorious experience that transformed the lives of ordinary men into something extraordinary, setting loose a mighty MOVE OF MIRACLES that shook the whole earth for Jesus Christ!

JESUS SENT ANOTHER COMFORTER

Now, when Christ walked among His disciples as their teacher, their example, and the One sent of the Father to show them what God is like, He was everything to them. He was the strength, the driving force, the power, the wisdom and the divine guidance for their lives. They could see with their own eyes and touch with their own hands the Man Who had walked the waters. They looked to Him, they depended upon Him completely, and He answered their cries. *He was their "Comforter."*

Actually, the word "Comforter" is a much stronger word than most of us have ever realized. It means "Strengthener." Strengthener! <u>"I am your Strengthener. I am your Comforter,"</u> Christ de-<u>clared.</u>

But the disciples were deeply troubled when He told them, "It is better for you that I, the Comforter, go away, because if I do not return to Heaven, the other Comforter will not come. But if I go, I will send you another Comforter, which is the Holy Ghost." (See John 14:16.)

On the day of Pentecost, these men from Galilee

received the promised Holy Spirit, the other Comforter, which in the Greek is translated "Paraclete, One called alongside to help." This powerful word "Paraclete" creates the imagery of a strong person standing by your side to help you over dangerous footing, or to lead you across a narrow and treacherous footbridge. So these disciples received the stronger One Who is called alongside to help, and that's exactly what it means to you and me today when we receive this real and dynamic experience in our lives!

The men and women who were gathered in the Upper Room that day were endued with supernatural power, power from on high! In the last chapter of Luke's Gospel, our Savior admonished them, "Go to the city of Jerusalem and tarry there until you are endued with power from on high." And in Acts 1:8 He also proclaimed, "But ye shall receiver power, after that the Holy Ghost is come upon you." Oh, glory be to God!

What kind of power is this Holy Ghost power? It's not of man's genius. It's not a man-induced power. It's not a power that's known by man through his mortal ways. It's a heavenly power! It's a limitless power that comes down to earth from a celestial realm into our lives! ***It's the spiritual demonstration of the pure energy of God!***

What does this power do? Its foremost purpose in the life of a believer is to empower you to be a bold witness for Jesus Christ. But it also fills you with the boldness and stamina you need to stand against the negative tides in the world around you — tides of sickness, fear, demons, poverty, loneliness, family disruptions.

> **THIS POWER ENHANCES EVERYTHING YOU ARE AND EVERYTHING GOD HAS CREATED YOU TO BE.**

For example, everyone is born with a special gift or talent, or perhaps more than one. Every man, woman and child has a calling to some ultimate destiny or purpose in this life. And <u>it's by releasing the power of the Holy Spirit through</u> ***praying in tongues with the understanding*** <u>that you can stir up that great gift and give it strength and force and vitality in your life!</u>

If you're a doctor, like my friend Bill, and you release the power of the Holy Spirit in your life, it can help you sharpen your gift and make you a better doctor. If you're a businessman or a farmer or a housewife or a teacher or a secretary (or whatever position you hold in life), God can enhance your talents and give you a fresh new outpouring of His power to do what He has called you to do!

I remember one woman who said, "My gift is to love my husband." And, oh, what a wonderful gift that is! How many men would like to be married to a woman like that? If that's the gift God has given you, then the power of the Holy Ghost will stir your heart to love your husband more than ever! And it will cause you husbands to love your wives better, too!

THE EXTRAORDINARY MIRACLES OF THE BIBLE WERE WROUGHT BY GOD'S SUPERNATURAL POWER

If we could only begin to fathom what it really means when the Scripture declares, *"Ye shall receiver power, after that the Holy Ghost is come upon you"* (Acts 1:8). It was God's supernatural power flowing through natural men that wrought the extraordinary miracles of the Bible: David slew the giant Goliath . . . Samson brought the temple of Dagon crashing to the ground as he defeated the Philistines . . . the three Hebrews escaped unharmed from the raging flames of Nebuchadnezzar's fiery furnace . . . Daniel was rescued from the jaws of the hungry lions . . . Peter and John miraculously raised up a lame man . . . Peter's shadow healed the sick . . . Paul, the apostle, shook the entire Gentile world with the message of the Gospel!

Not one of those incredible events could have been accomplished without these men becoming like conductors that carried a powerful voltage of electricity; but instead of carrying electrical current, *they were carrying the unlimited power of the Holy Spirit!*

You see, God's power is so formidable, so limitless, that when He stepped out onto nothing and simply spoke the Word, the earth was created. As He commanded the empty darkness of space to be filled with light, the sun and moon and stars streaked across the heavens. The earth itself was without form and void and it was flooded with water. As God spoke, "Let there BE," land began to heave forth from the billowy deep and the mountains, plains, deserts and hills were hurled into existence by the hand of God.

Then the Lord gathered the molecules and atoms of the dust into a mass and, when He breathed His power into that lifeless substance, man became a living soul. Really, when you think of the unlimited power of God to create something from nothing, you must realize that <u>our needs, regardless of how great they may be, how overpowering they may seem, can be ABUNDANTLY supplied when we're connected to God's unlimited power!</u>

IT'S GOD'S DESIRE
FOR YOU TO PLUG IN TO HIS POWER!

Friend, it's the Lord's desire for you to plug in to His unlimited, unending power through *praying in the Spirit with the understanding!* Or perhaps you've already released your prayer language, but you haven't been fully using this great gift God has given you, and you don't see His power operating in your life. I'll tell you, what you have available to you through the power of God's Spirit is like having a rare treasure in a locked room. But it's one thing to possess that treasure in a locked room, and it's another thing to FLING OPEN THE DOOR AND BRING THAT TREASURE FORTH!

This Christian life is designed to be a thrilling experience of power, with the Holy Spirit flowing through us as believers to perform the mighty works of Jesus. But yet in so many cases we Christians are filled with timidity, and this is a terrible, tragic thing. Terror strikes our hearts when we have the opportunity to witness for our Savior and we are intimidated when we try to believe for the healing of our bodies!

But with Holy Ghost power surging through our beings, a great fearlessness takes possession of us! We feel like we could lick a den of hungry lions! And, like those early Christians, we can proclaim the Word of God with boldness and not be intimidated in giving our testimony for the Lord. We will stop worrying about being eloquent. Besides, people are not looking for some kind of high-sounding orator. *They're looking for someone who has something real in his or her heart!*

THAT'S WHAT THIS WORLD IS DYING FOR, SOMEBODY WHO REALLY KNOWS JESUS!

I'll tell you, the power of God's Spirit will put within you a brand-new enthusiasm as a child of the Most High God! It will set your soul on fire until you can't stand still! It will flood your heart with the joy bells of Heaven and fill you with His glory until your cup overflows! *Then you'll just have to tell somebody about Jesus!* **And the Lord will send you into your world ON FIRE to win lost souls to His Son Jesus Christ!**

Chapter 7

"BUILD ME A UNIVERSITY!"

There are times when a man stands mute before the problems and challenges of his life. His heart is hungry for answers, but they seem to be so mysterious, so unreachable, as he wrestles with his own doubts and inner turmoil. The desire to accomplish his task becomes so big in his mind that it represents EVERYTHING he's ever wanted. But when he tries to pray, there's a dark cloud hanging over him, and his own human language breaks down in the face of the staggering issues that lie ahead.

He wonders, *What is God's will? How should I approach the Lord? What should I do? What should I say?* Then the Holy Spirit begins to flood from his innermost being and form words over his tongue, giving him utterance in a divine language, according to Romans 8:26. As he continues praying in his own earthly language, he can receive the interpretation back to his mind, as the Apostle Paul taught. (See I Corinthians 14:15.) And through this divine revelation, his mind blossoms, it's renewed, and God begins to show him how to accomplish the task that seems to be so incomprehensible.

I HAD NEVER REALIZED THERE WAS A DEEPER DIMENSION TO PRAYING IN TONGUES

It's a marvel to me how, for so many years after I had released my prayer language, I only prayed in tongues when I was in deep distress or when I got shouting happy, and a few phrases or syllables just flew out of my mouth! I never realized there was a deeper dimension to praying in tongues until I was faced with the mind-boggling task of building God a university.

You see, it was during my conversion that the Lord spoke to me and told me to build Him a university. When I received that mandate, I was on my way to be prayed for by a healing evangelist whose prayers released my body from the deadly grip of tuberculosis. I remember how I was lying there in the backseat of the car, listening to my brother Elmer's voice through the darkness, when suddenly his voice faded and I heard the Lord speaking directly to me, "Son, I'm going to heal you, and you are to take My healing power to your generation."

Now the world had never heard of a boy named

Oral Roberts from a little town called Bebee, Oklahoma, but God had marked the spot. And when He came into my presence that night He also whispered these words in my ear, "You are to build Me a university, based on My authority and the Holy Ghost."

I hadn't the slightest idea what those words meant, but I understood plainly that it was God speaking to me, that it was a revelation from on high. And when I talked about it later, people looked at me like I was somebody from outer space. No one believed me. Oh, perhaps my parents did, but I knew it was God Who had spoken!

Later, after traveling the globe with the Gospel of Jesus and taking His healing power to the far corners of the earth, those words were still burning in me like a fire shut up in my bones! And yet, when I stood face to face with that monumental task, I felt as if I could just as easily have taken a star and whirled it out through space as I could have built a university for the Lord!

IF YOU'VE EVER FELT ALONE AND HELPLESS, THEN I CAN IDENTIFY WITH YOU

I'm not ashamed to tell you that I cried out to God from the depths of my soul during those first few agonizing days and weeks after God told me His time had come for me to build His university. I

84

<u>wanted desperately to obey His voice, but I didn't
know how!</u> And it was out of my deep anguish and
bewilderment that I began walking back and forth
across the bare acres where Oral Roberts University
is now located, beseeching the Lord for the knowledge I needed to accomplish this great task.

Oh, I felt like I was carrying such a heavy load!
I was literally groaning and praying in English at
first, crying out, "O God, help me! Show me the
way!" Then, almost by accident, from the pit of my
belly, "the spirit language" rose up in me and just
rolled out of my mouth. When I stopped praying in
the Spirit, I started praying again, only this time the
words that came to me were in English and they
were certainly not words that I had thought of
myself. I felt such a tremendous release in my spirit
that I shouted, "Lord, let me do that again!"

I'll tell you, that was the most electrifying
experience I had ever had in my life! I was out there
all alone, with only the squirrels and rabbits and
birds as my audience, walking along praying in the
Spirit. When I stopped and listened again inside my
spirit, words came to me by the Spirit of God in
English, and *there was a brilliance to them.* Prophetic words were in my mouth — revelational
knowledge from the Lord!

And in those words, the Lord revealed to me the
most astonishing knowledge and He showed me the
broad outline of how to build Him a university. He

didn't give me all the details, but it was a great breakthrough into the knowledge and the ability of how to do what He had commanded me to do.

> **ONE THING I'VE LEARNED OVER THE YEARS IS NOT TO JUMP THE FIRST TIME YOU FEEL LIKE YOU'VE HEARD SOMETHING FROM THE LORD.**

What you hear in your spirit from the Lord must be tested by the Word of God and by the Spirit *and by practicality.* So, as I continued to seek the Lord over the next few weeks and months, the revelation He gave me was confirmed to my heart over and over again. I stepped out in faith with these words ringing in my soul: "I want you to build My university out of the same ingredient I used when I formed the world, when I created the earth — NOTHING."

All at once a Scripture from the book of Job flashed through my mind — "He [God] stretcheth out the north over the empty place, and hangeth the earth upon nothing" (Job 26:7). The Lord hung this earth upon empty space, upon NOTHING. And God reminded me of another Scripture in Hebrews 11:3 which says God framed the worlds by His word and used the things which we cannot see to make this visible world around us.

✳ Friend, that tells me that if you've ever felt like you had so little that you couldn't possibly make it for God, you can stop your worrying! **WITH GOD, you can do it, because the Bible says He calls the things that are not as though they were!** (See Romans 4:17.)

I'll never forget how I looked out across those empty acres much as the Lord Himself must have cast His eyes upon the empty spaces when He declared, "I have stretched My hand over the empty spaces and hung the world on nothing." And, in my mind's eye, when I looked at those bare grounds, I caught a glimpse of a university which was nothing yet, *but I could see it by faith.*

As I prayed in the Spirit with the understanding, God revealed to me that the Prayer Tower should be constructed at the center of ORU, at the very heart of the campus. The interpretation that came to me was, "Put the Prayer Tower in the center of academic learning," and that's exactly where we put it! Now the students have to pass by it as they walk from the dormitories to the library. There's no way around it! **Prayer and the power of God's Spirit are at the center of our academic life!**

"O GOD, DON'T LET ORAL
GO OFF THE DEEP END NOW!"

87

The very next morning after I first had this rich experience in the Lord, I was at home shaving and Evelyn overhead me praying in tongues and then talking to God in English. I was having such a glorious time that, finally, she couldn't stand it any longer so she peeked around the corner into the bathroom and exclaimed, "Oral, what on earth are you doing?"

"I'm shaving," I replied nonchalantly.

"That's not what I'm talking about," she murmured. "I've been hearing you do this all morning long and I want you to please tell me about it!"

So I began to explain to her about *praying in the Spirit with the interpretation* and she just looked at me blankly and sighed, "Oh, Oral, you've been so balanced all these years." Then she breathed a little prayer, *"O God, don't let him go off the deep end now!"*

I said, "Well, honey, all I know to tell you is that it's real, and now I know I'm going to build a university for God as He commanded me. I don't have all the details, but He's given me the broad outline."

No sooner had I finished shaving, than Evelyn popped her head back into the bathroom again and asked, "Oral, will you help me to better release my tongues?"

You see, we had never heard of the term "prayer language" and, really, it's a phrase that came to me that very morning from the Lord!

So I said, "Evelyn, this is the prayer language of the Spirit. Just raise your voice to the Lord and let it come pouring out!"

But she didn't know how to start, so I reminded her of what the Apostle Paul had said in I Corinthians 14:15: "I *will* pray with the spirit, and I *will* pray with the understanding also." "It's by your will," I told her. "You *will* to pray in the Spirit. Now I'm going to raise my voice and you join with me." All at once, two or three syllables came flowing out of her mouth, and then a few more, as together we began to pray and praise God in this new prayer language of the Holy Spirit.

Then I said, "Let's stop and listen, because the Lord is going to give us an interpretation back to our minds. Just begin to say out loud in English whatever you hear in your spirit."

Suddenly, the Holy Spirit welled up in her and she began to receive the interpretation from the Lord. I'll tell you, we sat there on the divan for several hours with our arms wrapped around each other, praying in the Spirit and listening for the interpretation until we were both tingling from our heads to our feet.

We came ALIVE in our prayer life — our two-way conversation with God — as never before! And we learned so much about tongues -- especially about how to interpret back to our minds *and* understanding in our own language, that I believe no two believers have ever had a more effective time in the Lord!

THIS HOLY GHOST EXPERIENCE IS LIKE ADAM LOOKING UP INTO THE EYES OF GOD ON CREATION MORNING

Friend, if you'll read the words of the Apostle Paul in I Corinthians 14:13-15, then you've got this experience of *praying in the Spirit with the understanding* in a nutshell!

> Wherefore let him that speaketh in an unknown tongue pray that he may interpret. For if I pray in an unknown tongue, my spirit prayeth, but my understanding is unfruitful. What is it then? I will pray with the spirit, and I will pray with the understanding also: I will sing with the spirit and I will sing with the understanding also.

Praying in tongues with the interpretation is like Adam looking up into the eyes of God on creation morning and declaring, "Hello, God," and God looking back at Adam and saying, "Hello, man."

"Hello, God. This is Oral."

"Well, hello, Oral. This is God."

Oh, can you take that in? It's really you and

the Lord in a private conversation! Oooooooh!

As I continued to put into practice this new revelation from God, I prayed in tongues all over that bare piece of ground in south Tulsa, Oklahoma! I was being obedient to the heavenly vision, calling that which was not as though it were. <u>And, right before my eyes, Oral Roberts University began to literally rise up from nothing to become a world-class university.</u>

Today, when I look around me, I see a miracle of miracles! I see a huge piece of land upon which there are many first-class buildings. I see a great faculty and thousands of handpicked, God-anointed students. We serve a first-class God, and we've built Him a first-class university based on His authority and on the Holy Spirit. And little by little we've received the acclaim of this nation's finest educators. Whether they've said it openly or privately, they've come to realize that *ORU is a jewel!*

Our students have the matchless opportunity of receiving an education for the whole man — spirit, mind and body — as the Lord directed us. First of all, they're developing their souls and their walk with the Lord, for God said to me, "Raise up your students to hear My voice, to go where My light is dim, where My voice is heard small, where My power is not known, even to the uttermost bounds of the earth. Their work will exceed yours and in that I am well pleased."

Not only are they developing their souls, but they're also developing their bodies through our widely acclaimed aerobics program as well as our athletics program, AND they're receiving a first-class academic education, developing their intellects and gaining the knowledge that will put them over in life!

You see, we do not reject knowledge, because <u>knowledge is of God</u>. In fact, the Bible says, "My people are destroyed for lack of knowledge" (Hosea 4:6). Oral Roberts University is not only a pioneer, spiritually speaking, but we are not ashamed to seek knowledge and truth wherever it is and whatever it is within the scope of our calling, and to excel in it and to be a light set on a great hill so that when people think of ORU, they think of great knowledge, great academic learning. At the same time, they think of the power of Almighty God, of our uncompromising stand on the Bible as the infallible Word of God *from beginning to end,* and of revelational knowledge by the Holy Spirit.

Oh, how many times was I told that it just couldn't be done! ***And I don't believe it could have been — nor could it continue — without PRAYING IN THE SPIRIT WITH THE UNDERSTANDING!***

"ORAL, GOD HASN'T CALLED ME
TO BUILD HIM A UNIVERSITY!"

Now you may be saying, "But, Oral, God hasn't called me to have a worldwide healing ministry or to build Him a university!" That may be true, but I believe there's SOMETHING He's called you to do and there's no one but you who can do it!

Besides, you should never be abashed or discouraged by thinking that what you're doing seems to be small or insignificant to God. The Lord wants you to be fully equipped to do whatever He has called you to do **so you can finish your course with great joy!** And, in my personal estimation, there is no way you can do that WITHOUT *praying in the Spirit and interpreting back to your mind, your understanding.* There's simply no substitute for it!

WITH THE POWER OF THE HOLY SPIRIT FLOWING THROUGH YOUR LIFE, PEOPLE WILL WANT WHAT YOU HAVE TO OFFER -- YOUR TALENTS, YOUR BUSINESS, YOUR EXPERTISE, YOUR WISDOM -- MORE THAN EVER BEFORE!

People came to hear me preach as a young man in 1947 in a gospel tent on North Main in Tulsa, Oklahoma, not because I was preaching about a dead God or a dead Bible or a dead, dry religious experience. It was the power of God's Spirit that made them flock to hear me, as a struggling young preacher coming out of these hills of eastern Oklahoma.

And when the Holy Ghost's power comes upon this little hunk of clay, there's a compassion that races through my being like a wind across a prairie and a fire that whips through my soul like a roaring inferno. A tenderness touches my heart like a mother pulling her crying baby to her breast and I want to reach out to the sick, the afflicted, the hurting, the demon possessed. I want to get at the thing that's hurting them, that's tearing them up and destroying them. I want every man, woman, boy and girl to be healed, ***AND THERE'S NO REST IN MY SPIRIT UNTIL THE HEALING COMES!***

And, my brother, my sister, God can put a brand-new fire in YOUR bones, a force in your inner man that will lift you up, that will thrust you into an even greater dimension of fulfilling His mighty calling on your life! Oh, don't be shy or hesitant! Just open yourself up to His Spirit! And don't you dare stop reading, because I've got so much more to tell you about the benefits of a talking God and a talking man engaging in a vibrant, two-way conversation by the Spirit!

It's like a mighty river flowing!

Chapter 8

MY OWN AND EVELYN'S PERSONAL HEALING FROM GRIEF

Evelyn realized immediately something was dreadfully wrong when she answered the doorbell early Saturday morning, February 12, 1977, and one of our faithful coworkers, Collins Steele, was standing at the back door with a policeman at his side. Collins opened up the morning newspaper and showed her the pictures of a horrible plane crash, and then he said softly, "Mrs. Roberts, we think it's Marshall and Rebecca."

His words just hung there in the chilly morning air. "Oh, those precious children!" Evelyn whispered as she shook her head in shock and disbelief. You see, Rebecca was our firstborn child and Marshall was her husband, and Evelyn knew their three little ones would be at home that very moment, so excited about their mommy and daddy coming home!

"Oral! Oral! Come quickly!" I heard her calling to me, and I knew by the sound of her voice that something wasn't right. When I rushed out to the kitchen, at first she just looked at me. She started telling me, but couldn't get through it. The policeman said, "Mr. Roberts, I've come to tell you that your daughter and son-in-law are dead."

"What happened?" I asked, looking over at Collins and the policeman incredulously.

Collins replied, "President Roberts, there was a plane that went down last night, and. . . ." Then he hesitated. "Well, there's a possibility that it isn't Marshall and Rebecca but, as far as we know, it is." Oh, I can't describe the hurt and the cry that ripped through my soul!

"Where did it happen?" I asked, and he told us how the plane had exploded over a wheatfield in Kansas, scattering our precious Marshall and Rebecca out there on that cold, lonely field, their bodies scarcely recognizable. Really, it was almost more than I could fathom.

My mind went back to the night Rebecca was born, and I thought about how I had been there at Evelyn's side when that little girl came out of her mother's body. She was a curly-haired, Indian-looking child, so beautiful, so strong, the only one of our four children who wasn't born in a hospital. *But now they were telling us she was gone.*

Evelyn and I just grabbed each other as the grief and horror swept over our souls. Then she whispered, "Honey, we've got to go to those three little children."

All the way over to Marshall and Rebecca's house, terrible questions were plaguing my mind. "God, why has this happened?" I cried. "Why? Why?" And then revelational knowledge rose up in my spirit from the Lord: *God knows something about this that we don't know.* How I clung to those words! I kept repeating them over and over again as I clutched Evelyn's hand tightly.

"GOD, YOU KNOW SOMETHING ABOUT THIS THAT WE DON'T KNOW."

We were surprised to find the children already awake that chilly Saturday morning. It turned out they had been up since seven o'clock and were gathered around the breakfast table, so happy to see us! We could scarcely choke back the tears as they rushed around us, hugging us and laughing, so we just sat down with them for a moment, desperately trying to contain ourselves. Then I asked Marcia, the eight-year-old, "Honey, why are you up so early this morning? You usually sleep late on Saturdays."

"Oh," she said brightly, "we got up early to see if our mommy and daddy were home yet!"

Friend, I felt like my insides were being torn apart as the grief and anguish welled up in my throat. Then I took those little ones in my arms and told them, "Your mommy and daddy won't be coming home again. We'll have to wait until we get to Heaven to see them the next time." I'll tell you, that was one of the most horrible moments of my entire life, as I told those little ones their mommy and daddy weren't coming home again! And I just grabbed Evelyn's hand and squeezed it as the tears burst from our eyes.

Then Brenda, the oldest, who was 13, reached down and picked up from the coffee table a little plaque which I had sent to all of my Partners. It said, "God is greater than any problem I have," and I remember how she hugged it tightly to her breast as the tears rolled down her cheeks.

And even though little Jon Oral, who was only five, didn't really grasp what was going on, he sensed in his childlike way that something was very wrong. I recall how he heard the cat crying later that night and he exclaimed, "The cat is crying because Mommy and Daddy aren't coming home!" His words sent shivers up and down our spines!

How could we possibly go on! How could we hope to make it through that first dark and lonely night as we wrestled with the thoughts of Marshall and Rebecca's bodies lying up there in that wheatfield in Kansas? I shuddered. In my mind I could see flashes of them, all battered and bruised, and I'd cry out and try to shake off those terrible images.

Not only that, but the devil began to mock me with a bitter, scorching fury. An accusing voice whispered, "You've been telling people there'll be a breakthrough from Heaven in '77. What do you have to say about it now?" and I burst into tears.

I felt so alone, but I gathered up my faith and hurled his words right back at him! ***"There will be a breakthrough from Heaven in '77!"*** I groaned, and I clung to those words with every fiber of my being!

SOMEHOW WE STRUGGLED THROUGH THOSE FIRST FEW DESPERATE HOURS

Somehow we managed to struggle through those first few desperate hours and then the first night passed. We were almost overwhelmed by all the decisions that faced us. Who would care for the children? Evelyn and I grappled with our own desire to take them, but we were in our late fifties and we felt like they needed someone younger than we were. Then it came to me how Marshall and Rebecca had talked about Marshall's brother, Bill, who was only a year or two older than Marshall, and his wife, Edna Earle, who was also Rebecca's best friend. They had mentioned if anything ever happened to them, Bill and Edna Earle should take the children.

As soon as we approached them about it, they agreed readily. "Oh, yes," they insisted. "We have been praying and God has impressed us to take them as our very own." So we all met together and gathered the five of them around us, and I took anointing oil and anointed them and prayed for God to put them together in the Lord as a brand-new family. We had the sweetest peace about that!

Over the next few days we were literally swamped with phone calls to the Prayer Tower and telegrams from our friends and Partners who had heard about our tragic loss, and slowly the reality of Marshall and Rebecca's deaths began to sink in on us.

At the funeral service, our student choir from Oral Roberts University sang the beautiful "Hallelu-jah Chorus" and I remember how, all of a sudden, I felt myself raising my left hand in the air in praise and worship to God. While those ORU students lifted their voices in praise and honor to the King of kings and Lord of lords, I just sat there with my hand upraised as waves of the Spirit washed over my soul.

I was completely unaware that anyone was watching me during that service, but later that night on one of our local television stations, the newscaster, a Jewish man who had attended the funeral, gave a little commentary.

He said, "When I saw Oral Roberts' left hand go up in the air, there was a warmth that flooded over me. Now, I'm not a Christian. I'm a Jew, but I understand that there's a God and I understand the 'Hallelujah Chorus.' I also believe his daughter and son-in-law are with God now, and I realize what it meant to him when he raised his hand during the singing of that great chorus."

<u>Friend, without this extraordinary spiritual experience of the other Comforter, the Holy Spirit, flowing through my life, there was no way I could have lifted my hand in praise and worship to God at a time like that!</u>

OH, THE NIGHTS ARE SO LONG!

In spite of our overwhelming grief and loneliness, Evelyn and I managed to stumble through those first few days and nights following the crash. But on the fourth night, I'll never forget how she came to me, crying, and said, "Honey, please pray with me in the Spirit. I've got to have some help or I feel like I'm not going to make it. This is the worst night yet and, oh, the nights are so long!"

So I took my darling in my arms and we began to pray in the Spirit, and the Lord gave us a word to strengthen us, "Remember, the mornings are so bright!" "The mercy of the Lord is new every morning." (See Lamentations 3:22,23.)

We just fell into each other's arms and began to cry and pray and groan and fumble our way through the rest of that prayer — "Oh, God, oooooooh!" — and the grief that struck us and grabbed us was indescribable.

We'd scream, "Why, God, why?"

Then Evelyn began to receive the first part of the interpretation: "For we wrestle not against flesh and blood, but against principalities, against powers, against the rulers of the darkness of this world. . . . Wherefore take unto you the whole armour of God . . . and having done all, to stand. Stand therefore. . . . *Praying always with all prayer and supplication in the Spirit*" (Ephesians 6:12-14,18).

> **GOD WAS TELLING US THAT THE SECRET TO OUR HEALING WAS IN *PRAYING IN THE SPIRIT WITH THE INTERPRETATION.***

And, believe me, when Evelyn and I were going through that time of deep, deep sorrow, if we had tried to get the grief out on our own, ***there's no way we would have made it!***

You see, with our minds we simply couldn't reach down deep enough inside us to get all of that anguish and heartache and bring it up and out.

102

And, oh, it was destroying us! But as we obeyed the interpretation the Lord gave us, the other Comforter, the Holy Spirit, was able to reach down and search out the hurts and bring all the pain and sorrow to the surface so He could heal our broken hearts!

As the Holy Spirit continued to flood up out of our souls that night, God gave me the rest of the interpretation. I said to Evelyn, "Honey, I feel like you and I are to go before the television cameras next Sunday and make a half-hour program and tell the people what's happened to us and how we hurt. There are terrible things wrong with people's lives today and they need to know they're not the only ones who've ever wrestled with grief and sorrow."

Then I whispered, "Honey, I really believe if we don't sow this as a seed to help others make it through their own desperate heartaches, this thing will haunt us and eventually kill our spirits. But if we'll do what the Lord is urging us to do, the Holy Spirit will enable us to face those TV cameras while we're crying our eyes out. And I believe we're going to help a whole lot of people who have had something precious snatched out of their lives just like we have."

"Oral, I can't do it!" Evelyn groaned. "I can't hold my hurt out for the whole world to see!"

"Well, I'll go alone," I assured her.

But she shook her head and sighed, "I won't

let you do it alone. I'll do it with you. I'll plant my seed, too."

That night as the Holy Spirit flowed through our souls, there were so many beautiful words that came to me. "God knows something about this that we don't know. Go to sleep, Evelyn. The angels are watching over you all night long. Go to sleep, my darling. God is going to heal our broken hearts." And those weren't just words. I mean, they were words that were anointed by the Holy Spirit, and Evelyn fell back on the pillow and went right to sleep!

Now it's a miraculous thing when you've lost a child and a son-in-law like we had and you can fall back on the pillow and go to sleep! Oh, I believe there was an angel nearby! I believe Heaven was bending low! And I know God's power was flowing through us so strongly because we were *praying in the Spirit with the understanding!*

WE LET OUR GRIEF HANG OUT
FOR THE WHOLE WORLD TO SEE

Friend, let me tell you, it was hard for Evelyn and me to hold our heads up that day as we faced those television cameras and let our grief hang out for the whole world to see. Surrounded by baskets and baskets of telegrams and letters of condolence that had come pouring in from across the nation and around the world, we sat there in that little studio with the tears rolling down our cheeks and told our heartbreaking story.

I reminded our friends and Partners that I had always opened my telecast each week by declaring, "Something good is going to happen to you!" And I announced to the whole world that I was still proclaiming those very same words, believing that the Christ of the Resurrection would bring us out into the sunshine again, with the joy of the Lord in our souls!

Then we told them about the awful grief and anguish that had gripped our hearts when we first heard the news of Rebecca and Marshall's deaths, and how we had wept as we gathered our three little grandchildren in our arms and told them their mommy and daddy weren't coming home again. <u>But we declared that our faith was in a God Who is deeply involved in our hurts and our losses, and we believed He would bring us through!</u>

Oh, how we felt our spirits soar as we began to praise and thank God that we knew where Rebecca and Marshall were — safe in the arms of Jesus in Heaven! But then I heard myself saying, "Evelyn, there are people all over the world who have lost loved ones and some of them are wondering right now, 'Is my son, my daughter, my mother, my father, in Heaven?'"

As I looked into those TV cameras, I told the

people, "When Jesus, our Savior, hung on the cross, there were two other men who were crucified nearby. They were thieves — vicious, cruel men — seemingly without much hope for salvation. But, in a moment's time, one of those men had a change of heart. He cried out to the living Christ, and the Lord said, '*Today shalt thou be with me in paradise*' (Luke 23:43). You know, it doesn't take a long time for a man or a woman or a boy or a girl to give their heart to Jesus. You never know about your loved one. How can you be sure that right before they drew their last breath, they didn't call upon the Lord?"

When the cameras were turned off that day, we knew we had sown a powerful seed to our God, believing for Him to bring us up out of the valley VICTORIOUSLY! And as we beamed that program by television all across this nation and Canada, we were reaching out to people who needed a healing from a heart that was torn, from a body that was grieving, from eyes that were flowing with tears. And through our faith in a Christ Who is alive forevermore, we proclaimed that out of the ashes of Rebecca and Marshall's deaths there would arise a great glory.

When our associates gathered around us in that little television studio, we suddenly felt the dark clouds begin to lift. We told them, "Even though death may brush our lives for a brief moment, there's going to be a resurrection from the dead." And we could feel the power of God's Spirit bringing Heaven a little closer **as the power of the Resurrection began to burst alive in our hearts!**

It was like a mighty river flowing!

Chapter 9

HOW GOD HEALED MY BROKEN HEART THROUGH THE PRAYER AND PRAISE LANGUAGE OF THE SPIRIT

by Evangelist Terry Law

A PERSONAL WORD OF INTRODUCTION

Terry Law is one of the first graduates of Oral Roberts University and a strong supporter of this healing ministry. For several years now we have had the honor of having Terry serve as a member of the ORU Board of Regents.

While Terry was still a student at ORU, he founded a very powerful music ministry group known as Living Sound. Not only did they minister throughout this country, but Terry's bold vision involved taking the Gospel of Jesus Christ to places behind the Iron Curtain and eventually even to Russia.

Through the years I have watched with great pride as the fulfillment of Terry's dream has come to pass. Because of his determination and obedience to God, Living Sound did indeed minister many times behind the Iron Curtain and in Russia, long before any of us believed Russia would turn against godless communism and come to the very edge of its own disintegration.

The first evangelical minister to be carried live on nationwide TV in Russia was Terry Law, and it was Terry and his group Living Sound who, more than any others, have put their lives on the block to open Russia to the Gospel.

Terry Law is a man I greatly admire. When I heard, several years ago, of the sudden and tragic loss of his dear wife and the terrible time he was going through, I knew there was no way this young man would be able to go on without the healing power of the Holy Spirit flooding through his life.

So I called Terry and made an appointment to talk with him. When we met, I really poured out my heart to him and shared out of my own tragic experiences with loss. Here in Terry's own words is his account of what happened in our meeting, and what has happened in his life as a direct result of his coming into a deeper understanding of the prayer and praise language of the Spirit.

--Oral Roberts

"LORD, THIS ISN'T FAIR!"

I was aroused from a deep sleep by someone shaking me, whispering, "Terry, I have some terrible news!" I looked up into the tear-stained face of my associate, David Weir, his eyes full of anguish, but it was his words that shattered my world that fateful night!

"Terry, we've just received news that your wife has been killed in an automobile accident."

"Oh," I groaned, and then I turned away and shuddered as the thought of Jan's death chilled me to the bone. "No, there's got to be some mistake!" I argued. The thoughts raced through my mind in rapid-fire succession. *How could she possibly be gone? I just spoke with her yesterday from JFK Airport on my way to England. This must be some kind of awful nightmare!*

Dazed and stunned, I tried to shake off this grim new reality, but somehow I couldn't shake it. What about our children? Oh, I ached to be with them, to feel them wrap their arms around me!

A few moments later, when I heard their voices on the other end of the telephone, I felt like my heart would burst into pieces! How could they possibly grasp this horrible news when I could barely comprehend it myself? They were so brave, so strong, and yet talking to them only made Jan's death seem so cold, so final.

On that long flight home to Tulsa, the grief began to fasten its deadly grip on me. "Lord," I cried bitterly, "this isn't fair! I've done everything I know to do to share the Gospel all around the world. I've been interrogated by the KGB on my trips to Russia five different times. Why has something like this happened to me?" But there was only a cold silence that crept over me like a fog, and it was broken only by the terrible sobs that convulsed my body.

After Jan's funeral, I felt myself sinking into a despair that seemed to swallow me up. A fierce loneliness haunted me day and night, and I was plagued by questions that were tearing me apart. It was staggering to me that God would allow something like this to happen after I had served Him with every fiber of my being for all these years! Bitterness rose up in me like an enormous wall, and it seemed as if nothing and no one could break through it.

Then, about a month after Jan's funeral, Oral Roberts and I arranged a time to meet together. I knew that he and his family had just come through a time of deep waters, having lost a daughter and son-in-law and also their oldest son within the span of only a few short years. If anyone could identify with the gut-wrenching heartache and the emptiness I was feeling, I knew Oral could.

There in his office we knelt together and prayed. Hot, bitter tears stung my face as I poured out my heart to him. And after he had listened carefully to every word, he began talking with me out of his own shattering experiences with loss.

As I was leaving, he spoke the most powerful word I believe anyone has ever spoken to a human being who needed the courage to go on. He said, "Terry, I want you to go home and get on your knees and start to pray in the Spirit; start to praise the Lord."

Immediately a sinking feeling struck me in the pit of my stomach. "I can't do it!" I moaned in bewilderment, and I felt that same heartsickening feeling beginning to well up in me again.

"Terry, you've got to," he insisted gently.

Then he pointed out the window at the Prayer Tower on the Oral Roberts University campus and asked me, "Do you see that?" I nodded numbly, wondering what on earth the Prayer Tower had to do with the overwhelming feeling of loneliness which was threatening to engulf me.

"Terry, everything you see before you on this campus was birthed in me first by praying in the Spirit and then by receiving the interpretation from the Lord back to my mind."

"But, Oral," I exclaimed in desperation, "how is that going to help me face the future without Jan?"

"That's the *only* way Evelyn and I could have made it through the heartbreaking losses of our children," he said. "If we hadn't *prayed in the Spirit with the interpretation,* we would never have known that out of the rubble God could bring a great miracle."

I knew Oral had already traveled that lonesome valley, but it was so hard for me to grasp that <u>something as simple as *praying in the Spirit with the understanding* could wash away the brutal pain that was gnawing at me.</u> I thanked him and walked away feeling completely helpless, like there was really no way I could do what he had asked me to do. I still felt so dazed and numb and, besides, **he had actually told me to PRAISE THE LORD!** How could I ever praise Him again after everything that had happened! I shuddered.

WHEN I TRIED TO PRAISE THE LORD, THE WORDS KEPT FLYING BACK IN MY FACE

Early the next morning, I staggered out of bed and, when I started trying to praise God, the words kept flying back in my face. I could literally feel the devil sitting on my shoulder as I whispered in a halting way, "Praise the Lord. Glory to God. Hallelujah." Those words sounded so empty and meaningless!

Then the devil began to sneer accusations at me: "Well, what are you praising the Lord for? Your wife is dead!"

But I just kept on saying, "Bless Your Name,

Lord! Thank You, Jesus!"

Then he piped up again, "Thank Him for what? Because you've got three little children now who don't have a mother?"

After about fifteen more minutes of that kind of dialogue, I was ready to throw up my hands and quit. But, all of a sudden, out of my spirit rose these words from Psalm 34:1: *"I will bless the Lord at all times: his praise shall continually be in my mouth."*

Something clicked in me when I remembered those few words of Scripture, even though they seemed so bittersweet as I said them through my tears. I just set my jaw and cried, "God, I don't understand this and I may never understand it, but I know one thing. YOU ARE WORTHY TO BE PRAISED!" Then I declared, ***"And I will praise You!"***

Even though I knew those words had come bursting from the depths of my heart, I felt like a drowning man about to plunge beneath the waves for the last time, and I was grabbing frantically for a rope. <u>Somehow I got hold of that single strand of praise and I hung on for dear life.</u>

For about an hour, it seemed like nothing much happened . . . only the same dull ache throbbing in the pit of my stomach. But, after about two and a half hours, I suddenly felt something building up inside me like a roaring wall of water about to hurtle over a dam! In the next instant, I felt my soul exploding deep within me and I began to pray in the Spirit and I knew I was breaking through to God!

Then, for the first time in my life, I began to receive the interpretation back to my mind, as Oral had urged me to do. All at once, I began prophesying to myself, and I commanded the anger to GO! I commanded the self-pity to GO! <u>And when I rose up off my knees that day, that horrible aching feeling in the pit of my stomach had vanished and an incredible healing had begun in my heart!</u>

The very next night, as I was holding my children close to me and we were all praying and crying out to the Lord, their little bodies began to heave and they began to sob almost uncontrollably — as though their hearts would break in two. "Misty, Scotty, 'Becca, let's pray in the Spirit," I whispered, and those brave little ones began praying in their prayer languages along with me. After a few minutes, we began to praise and worship the Lord together. Then I asked God to let me interpret our prayers and, as the interpretation came, the Lord began to pour His powerful healing balm over our wounds as He mended the broken pieces of our little family!

"IN THE DARKEST HOUR OF YOUR LIFE
I HAVE TAUGHT YOU
TO PRAISE AND WORSHIP ME."

It was only a few short months later, as I continued my "sacrifice" of praise and worship to the Lord each day (including *praying in the Spirit with the interpretation*), that I had an unforgettable experience with the Lord. In the midst of my prayer, I felt an electrifying awareness of the power of God and His presence suddenly filled the room.

Through the interpretation that followed, I felt God speaking to me, giving me a very strong word concerning the future of my ministry: "Terry, in the darkest hour of your life I have taught you how to truly praise and worship Me. Now I want you to begin to lead My people in praise and worship. As you obey Me, I will heal the sick and deliver those who are oppressed with demon spirits. And you will see more people saved through your ministry than you have ever seen before."

All at once, I felt something brand new stirring deep inside me -- a sharpened sense of purpose and a new direction for my life's work. My ministry team and I began to lead people into the presence of the Lord through praise and worship, and we watched in complete astonishment as the power of the Holy Ghost fell and God performed extraordinary miracles!

During the time the Lord was healing my family and me from our own gut-wrenching pain and sorrow, I saw God shatter the chains of oppression and sickness and torment in the lives of the people to whom we ministered. <u>It was through this deeper dimension of praise and worship that a great new wave of God's power was released through my ministry.</u> And because of what Oral Roberts taught me about *praying in the Spirit with the interpretation*, God has miraculously revolutionized my entire life!

A FINAL WORD ABOUT TERRY LAW

I am so grateful to God for Terry's healing from grief and the revelational knowledge the Lord has given him for his life and ministry. That in itself would be a happy ending to this story. But even better than that, some time later, Terry met a precious lady named Shirley. She had lost her husband and had two children of her own that she was trying to raise alone. Together, Terry and Shirley now have a wonderful marriage, a blended family and a child from their own union, and God is using both of them mightily as a husband-and-wife team in the healing ministry of Jesus Christ.

Currently, Terry is responsible for supplying millions of Bibles and New Testaments to the Russian people. For the past 20 years, he has been perhaps the single best-known and best-received individual minister of the Gospel in that country (the former Soviet Union). Even now, after the long years of persecution, danger and risk to his own life, he has continued to move deeper and deeper into Russia in its present chaotic condition.

And I must tell you one thing more. When Terry graduated from ORU in 1970 and shared his call and vision with me for the Iron Curtain countries and Russia, he asked if I would help him pursue his life's work. I started to say, "Of course, Terry. After all, you're one of my graduates whom God told me to raise up to go where His light is dim, His voice is heard small, His power is not known, even unto the uttermost bounds of the earth. Your work will exceed mine and in that God is well pleased."

But the Holy Spirit checked me. Under my breath I began to pray in the Spirit and interpret back to my mind and God gave me the following answer, which I related to Terry.

"If there's anyone I would be willing to help in his or her special calling, and especially to go into Russia with the Gospel, it would be you. I've watched you grow here at ORU and seen the ability God has given you and the faith and determination you have in your heart to obey the Lord with your education and your life.

"But the Spirit has just informed me that if I, Oral Roberts, help you at this time, you will be tempted to look to me as your source, instead of God, and it will weaken you and you will fail.

"I must go against my own desires and tell

you no in order that you will do what I have done: obey God regardless of how hard it is, how lonely you may get, how much danger you face, and how you have to use your faith as a seed you sow, trusting God for miracle harvests. Someday, when God releases me, I will help you to the extent He leads me. For now I sense in my spirit you must strike out by faith alone and see what God will do through your life."

Later Terry said that was one of the greatest lessons he had ever learned. As we prayed together that day and he left to travel the road to his own God-ordained destiny, it seemed as if he had reached the end before he had even begun. However, over the years I was constantly hearing about Terry Law and Living Sound (composed mostly of fellow ORU graduates) traveling into the Iron Curtain countries and finally into Russia itself.

When I learned of the KGB interrogations, I realized what that meant. But when I heard that the Russian television network was carrying Terry and Living Sound LIVE throughout the entire nation, I realized this was the first breakthrough to what was coming in the future, and I knew I had done the right thing in following God's direction to let him go by his own faith.

When God finally released me to help Terry, I did so in every way I could. It has paid off in tens of thousands of souls won to Christ, countless numbers of healings, and in knowing that God had to have a Terry Law who was willing to go it alone at first and trust the Lord to do with him as He would. And I believe Terry's experience with the *prayer language of the Spirit with the interpretation* is another strong witness to the power of the Holy Spirit to guide and comfort His people through all the tragedies and heartaches of this present life.

Chapter 10

THE PRAYER LANGUAGE OF THE SPIRIT WITH THE UNDERSTANDING: GOD'S SUPERNATURAL TRACKING SYSTEM

When the trials of life come rolling in on you like a cyclone roaring across the prairie, like a shooting star racing across the heavens, like the blow of a hard fist striking you on your jaw, it can knock you flat on your back, literally taking your breath away. And as you're lying there, reeling from the terrible impact, the grueling pain, the aloneness, there appears to be no power on the horizon which has the force to set you on your feet again, let alone to lift you up from the lowest pit to the highest Heaven.

Throughout my 75 years here on this earth, I've scaled some of life's loftiest mountains and struggled through some of the deepest valleys, but the second critical blow which struck my life (the first being my bout with tuberculosis) caught me totally off guard. On October 6, 1992, while being driven back to my room after preaching live on Trinity Broadcasting Network in Tustin, California, a sharp pain ripped through my left side, stabbing at me relentlessly.

By the time I reached the room, the pain was raging like nothing I had ever known before and, all at once, I hit the floor, unconscious, suffering from a massive heart attack. My darling wife, Evelyn, heard me and dialed 911 and the next thing I knew, the paramedics were rushing me to Hoag Memorial Hospital in Newport Beach, California. In one fleeting moment, it seemed as if my supernatural tracking system with God had somehow been cut off, and I had lost my footing. I felt as if I were floundering in the dark, in a shadowy world where I had somehow lost my way.

Over the last few lonely hours, as I drifted in and out of consciousness, my body was revived and snatched from the clutches of death itself four times. During that experience, I received a revelation from the Lord that has helped me in an extraordinary way, and I believe it will be invaluable to you in your own life. I know it's one of the most profound things God has ever shown me about *the prayer language of the Spirit with the understanding,* which I'm also calling GOD'S SUPERNATURAL TRACKING SYSTEM.

What do I mean by God's supernatural tracking system? In Psalm 18:33, the Psalmist David puts his finger on the key issue when he declares, "He [God] maketh my feet like hinds' feet, and setteth me upon my high places." I'll tell you, when that heart attack roared down on me like a fierce wind whipping through my body, I felt like I was in the lowest of the lowlands — not in the high places of God!

Now in order for you to fully comprehend what this scripture means for your life, you must understand that the hind, as described in this psalm and in other passages in the Bible, is the female red deer, and God has fashioned this creature in an especially unique way, unlike all the rest of His creation.

The hind appears to be the most correlated of all the animals God created, because she has a special tracking system built into her being. Her back feet track so perfectly with her front feet that when she hits the ground with her front feet, her back feet follow in perfect unison, landing in exactly the same spot, *without missing an inch.*

The hind's body, her inner self, her instincts, and whatever mind or intellect an animal possesses, are all so perfectly coordinated that she can run with abandon, leaping surefootedly over the rough, rugged terrain as she races with the wind! Whether she's bounding through the lowlands or turning her head to the high places, scaling the sides of a steep precipice, hurtling over mountain ledges or sharp rocks jutting from the walls of a narrow mountain pass, she leaps with wild abandon to the high places where God sets her, *and He alone can set her there!*

The Lord designed this wonderful creature this way because she bears the responsibility for her young, and she must find a special hiding place far removed from the dangers lurking down below, where she can camouflage herself, bear her young, and bring them safely back down the mountain.

As she races toward the heights, taking her little ones with her, she doesn't have to worry about plunging to her death because she knows her tracking system is flawless. She can turn her face to the wind and race with wild abandon to the inner recesses of her high places, where she can hide her young and **NO ENEMY CAN FIND HER!**

I never fully appreciated how vital an animal's tracking system is until I went on my first deer hunt in Colorado many years ago. It was early in the season, and we quickly discovered that the deer were still high up in the mountains, so we rented horses to carry us up the steep slopes.

About halfway there, the horses balked and refused to go another step. Why? Because their tracking system is not as perfect as the deer's. Their hind feet miss the spot where their front feet hit the ground by over 3 to 4 inches. Those horses instinctively sensed that it was far too treacherous for them to make that steep climb up to the higher slopes. So they halted dead in their tracks, and we had to ride back down the mountain without even firing a shot!

Through that experience, I discovered something very remarkable about the hind, the female deer. THAT SPECIALLY DESIGNED CREATURE DOES NOT HAVE TO STOP ANYWHERE! She can run with the fiercest stormy blast, through high places and low, skipping over the rocks and boulders, perfectly coordinated, knowing that her tracking system is so flawless that she will not stumble!

Therefore, she can run — number one, with ABANDON; and number two, she can run with MOMENTUM. Really, if you think about it, momentum is the secret of the Christian life, because God did not create us to live at the bottom of the heap, to be trampled underfoot by the devil. He made us to rise to the top, to soar with the wind, to be the head and not the tail! (See Deuteronomy 28:13.)

God built within us a supernatural tracking system so we can run this race with faith, hope and confidence, not cowering in fear that we'll stumble or that the enemy will overpower us. He's put within us an inner tracking system by His Holy Spirit that gives us **SUPERNATURAL MOMENTUM** — the type of momentum that the hind possesses through her unique tracking system!

Friend, as I lay there on that hospital bed, hovering between life and death, engulfed by an awful feeling of helplessness, MY MOMENTUM HAD COME TO A STAGGERING HALT! But the Lord took me to this verse in Psalm 18:33 and, like a bolt of lightning, the words of that psalm lodged in my consciousness with mighty force: **"HE MAKETH MY FEET LIKE HINDS' FEET, AND SETTETH ME UPON MY HIGH PLACES."**

In my spirit, I suddenly caught a glimpse of myself running with abandon again! Oh, how my heart was craving to turn my face to the wind and RUN WITH IT! My spirit was racing within me, ready to run with the momentum of God, looking to Him to set me upon my high places!

HOW THE DEVIL'S "UPSET" CAN SHATTER YOUR MOMENTUM

There's a classic story that's lived in my heart all through the years, about a thoroughbred race-horse named Man O' War who captured the hearts of Americans everywhere many years ago. I've traveled to Lexington, Kentucky, where this great racehorse is buried, and I've seen his statue — a deep, rich red color — the image of a high-spirited horse with a flying mane and tail.

Samuel D. Riddle was Man O' War's owner, and when he saw this colt with its deep, rich red color, kicking up its heels as it sped across the pasture with a stride like he had never seen before, he exclaimed to his grooms, "Watch that colt! Take care of that colt! I'm going to name him Man O' War!"

Throughout his entire racing career, Man O' War lost only one race. He had such incredible momentum that once he burst through the starting gate, he never broke stride until he shot across the finish line. When he galloped around the track with his tail flying and his mane whipping in the wind, there was no horse that could even stand in his shadow! He ran like a streak of lightning, winning race after race, hands down (sometimes by as many as ten lengths), and he went on to become America's favorite racehorse.

Near the end of Man O' War's racing career, in one race, the owners of all the other horses made a deal with their grooms and jockeys that when they got within 200 yards of the finish line, they would close in on Man O' War and break his momentum before he could turn on that last flash of speed for the finish. They knew the only way they could tear the prize away from that great racehorse was to stop his momentum, and that's exactly what they did!

Those who were watching the race that day declared it so enraged Man O' War when those horses surrounded him that he raised his proud head, with his nostrils flared, and almost reared up as he turned to the right and then to the left, struggling wildly to regain his momentum as he finally burst through the throng. But in spite of his daring spirit, Man O' War lost that race by a nose to a little upstart horse named UPSET!

Oh, friend, this is no fairy tale! It actually happened, and it's a startling reminder that UPSET is not much until it deals you a blow in your own life! When things are upset and your life is brutally invaded by satan, as mine was through that massive heart attack -- when the enemy forces come barreling down on you and you're knocked flat on your back physically or mentally or emotionally or spiritually or financially and you cannot seem to regain your momentum -- then UPSET becomes an awful thing to face!

KING DAVID FACED
A MONUMENTAL UPSET IN HIS LIFE

When God set David on the throne of Israel, the whole nation was in terrible disarray. The first king, whose name was Saul, had disgraced himself and sinned against God. He had broken faith with the people, and the entire country was left vulnerable to the onslaughts of its most bitter enemies.

But when David took the throne, *he was aware that God had made his feet as hinds' feet and had set him in his high places* and, as king, he achieved a

128

greater correlation with the Lord than any man had ever done before. His spirit, mind, body, and attitude were so much like God's that the Lord Himself proclaimed he was "a man after His own heart" (I Samuel 13:14)!

Hebrew scholars tell us that David was physically the best-coordinated man in Hebrew history. In Psalm 18:34 he boasts that God had given him such remarkable strength that he could break bands of steel with his bare hands. Can you imagine a man taking steel rods in his hands and breaking them into pieces! Well David was such a mighty man of war that he could burst asunder great bands of steel with his bare hands!

King David was also the man who first drove back the borders of Israel and thrust out her enemies, conquering the buffer nations between Israel and all her enemy lands. Then he reunited the Hebrew nation, joining under his rule the ten northern tribes with the southern tribes of Judah and Benjamin. And during David's reign, Israel became the wealthiest and most powerful nation in the world -- *all because her king had correlated his life with God!*

Not only did David accomplish all those mighty feats but he also built a house -- not a physical house of wood or stone but a house of faith called the House of David. With his wife, he brought forth a child, and through his lineage the baby Jesus was born in the City of David, Bethlehem of Judea. David finally climbed to his high places in Christ when our Savior was called THE SON OF DAVID!

David was a man who was so totally correlated with God and had such astonishing momentum that it was no great challenge for him to face the lion and the bear. (See I Samuel 17:34-36.) Really, it was a once-in-a-lifetime challenge for the lion and the bear to face the young shepherd boy!

And when David stood there in the valley of Elah, staring up at the terrible glistening armor of Goliath, the champion of the Philistines, the giant roared with laughter at this puny little boy who was flinging a slingshot around his head. But young David was so correlated and his feet were so much like hinds' feet, that he **took care of Goliath's head SPEEDILY!** (See I Samuel 17:45-58.)

DAVID'S UPSET CAME WHEN HE FAILED TO STAY WITHIN HIS CALLING

David encountered a heartbreaking upset in his life when he failed to stay within his calling as the soldier-leader of the armies of Israel. Early in the spring of the year, when all the kings went out to battle, he made an ill-fated decision to remain in Jerusalem and take his ease in the palace. (See II Samuel 11, 12.)

Late one night as he was gazing out across the

city, he saw his neighbor's wife, Bathsheba, bathing on a nearby rooftop. She was very beautiful, so he sent for her and they committed adultery. To the king it must have seemed a small thing to take another man's wife. But then he engineered the brutal death of her husband, and who could do anything about it? There was an invisible law which seemed to gloss over matters like that.

In the sweep of a moment, David's correlation with God was shattered, his supernatural tracking system was cut off, and his momentum was broken, until one day the Prophet Nathan arrived at the palace. The Bible says Nathan told David this little parable about a rich man who was being visited by friends.

It seems a certain rich man had great possessions and huge flocks with thousands of sheep and goats. He could have slaughtered any of them to feed his house guests. Instead, he went over to a poor man's house, seized his only little lamb and slew it, and barbecued it for dinner.

"What should be done with a man like that?" the Prophet Nathan asked.

"He should be killed!" David shouted with indignation.

It must have been an electrifying moment when Nathan whispered, "O king, thou art the man."

He was really saying, "David, you had *every-*

thing. Then you stole another man's wife, and to cover up your crime, you maneuvered him into a position in battle where it was certain he would be slaughtered."

Oh, my, the correlation between David and the Lord had vanished! His momentum had come to a standstill. And now the man whose hands could break the bands of steel could barely even lift his hands at all. The Bible says David fell on his face before the Lord and repented and wept bitterly, and God restored his supernatural tracking system and set him again on his high places!

WHEN WE EXPERIENCE AN UPSET, WE CAN GO IN ONE OF TWO DIRECTIONS

When an upset rips through our lives and plunges us into deep and dangerous waters, there are two directions we can go. If it's not our fault, as in the case of Man O' War (and as it was in my own case when I was struck down by a massive heart attack), there may be a fleeting moment when we lose by a nose, but on the whole WE WILL WIN.

However, if the upset comes because we've committed a sin that breaks our wholeness, that casts a shadow on our relationship with God, then "the prophet will deliver the message" and there will be no escaping the word. You see, the Lord loves us so much that He always sends His prophets with a word to deliver us from the deadly grip of our sins. It doesn't matter whether they're a pastor, an evangelist, a singer, or a lay person, if the prophetic power is upon them, they're sent from God to lift us up out of the quagmires of satan's efforts to destroy us.

When the prophet delivers the word, it will pierce straight through our hearts, and we'll have an opportunity either to make it right or to try to "live with it." If we try to live with it, then we'll never rise again to our high places in Christ Jesus. We'll never regain our momentum for God in this world if we live to be a million years old!

If you're reading my words today and you've lost your correlation with God, your supernatural tracking system has been interrupted, your momentum has come to a halt, and a coverup has been erected, *know that you cannot win.* **YOU WILL LOSE.** Your vision for your life will perish and your very soul will be lost forever unless you make things right with the Lord!

But the good news is, if you repent as David did, God will make your feet like hinds' feet once again, and He'll set you on your high places! *And only God can set you there!* You cannot set yourself in those high places, and man cannot set you there. When the Lord sets you in your high places, you are in your own realm. It's a place in God that becomes eternal, never to be uprooted by mortal man!

Friend, your place doesn't belong to anyone else in the whole world! There's no one else who can sing your song or preach your sermon or pray your prayer or love your wife or your husband or run your business or fulfill your calling — NO ONE BUT YOU! You're special to the Lord, and He's put within you a supernatural tracking system that's perfect — *the prayer language of the Spirit with the understanding.* Really, we can overcome every evil thing that lashes out at us through our supernatural tracking system because Jesus Christ came to restore our lost tracking system and to make our feet as hinds' feet and establish us in our high places!

WHEN THE UPSET COMES HURTLING INTO YOUR LIFE, IT'S JUST YOU AND GOD!

I know the Lord began to restore His tracking system in my own life that fateful night last October when I was struggling so desperately to shake off the effects of the anesthesia. Lying there in that dimly lit hospital room, I felt like I was trapped in a thick fog. Occasionally, I caught a glimpse of shadows shuffling back and forth in front of me as the doctors and nurses were coming and going, and the sound of their voices drifted toward me like faint, faraway whispers.

All at once I was keenly aware that no matter

how many specialists were hovering over me, Oral
Roberts was truly alone, and the reality of it struck
me with stunning force. When the upset comes
hurtling into your life with the force of a meteor,
then it's just you and God alone!

As that horrible feeling of aloneness swept over
my soul and seemed to fill my hospital room, I
glanced around me in the darkness and saw the
heart pump, the respirator, and every tube imagin-
able hooked up to my body. The tubes running
down my nose and throat were lodged so close to my
voice box that I couldn't even talk. And, oh, how I
longed to say something!

Then out of the depths of my being the questions came floating up in my consciousness, and I
began to ponder how the man who had proclaimed
that God is a good God and had laid his hands upon
such a great multitude of people to pray for their
healing could suddenly be gripped with the feeling
that the Lord was a million miles away!

I was angry and hurting and in my spirit I cried
out, "O God, why has this happened to me? I
haven't been a perfect man, but I've always had a
heart for You. I've served You, Lord. I've walked in
Your path. I've loved Your Name and cared about
people — the lost, the desperately ill, the demon
possessed, those who've been kicked aside by life.
What have I done to deserve this?"

Now those were not the right questions, but for

a split second, in my utter frustration, I reeled off that litany that we all go through about how we've served God and we've planted our seeds of faith. And, when I was finished, I was looking pretty good to myself! But all those high-sounding words didn't faze the master spirits of the devil one bit. They just kept on roaring at me as they executed their deadly assault!

But there were even more questions looming up in front of me, much more serious questions. After all, I had already lived 74 years here on this earth and had spent over 45 years in the healing ministry. I had built a first-class university for God and was preparing to turn the reins of Oral Roberts University over to the second president.

My life was in order, so the question I was really grappling with was, *"Do I want to live?"* And that may be the fiercest question you or I will ever tackle when we're struck by an upset of serious proportion. "Do I want to continue? Do I want to step aside? Do I want to die? Do I want to go on to Heaven now? Is God through with me? Is this my time to die?"

Well, asking those questions wasn't difficult, but the consequences of asking them were colossal *because I was alone.* I was not only *alone,* but there was a soul-shaking feeling of *aloneness* that flooded through my being that night, because my supernatural tracking system with God had been cut off.

My momentum had been broken, and I was fighting an agonizing battle for consciousness, for lucidity, and, above all, for UNDERSTANDING!

YOU AND I MUST LEARN TO PRAY
FROM THE RIVER —
NOT FROM THE CHIN UP
AND NOT FROM THE LIPS!

While I was down in that dark, deep place, the light of God's Word suddenly splintered the darkness, and I reached out in my spirit and grabbed hold of the verse in Ephesians 6:18: "Praying always with all prayer and supplication IN THE SPIRIT."

For the first few moments, the words of that scripture were like a hammer pounding away at me to pray in the Spirit, but I couldn't even talk! I couldn't bring a sound up, so I felt like there was no way I could pray at all!

Then, like a flash, my mind went back to the times I had crossed the deserts of this great nation and had seen dry river channels carved among the desert sands. Most of the year those rivers aren't flowing, as the dry riverbeds await the coming rain. But even then, on each side along the riverbanks, everything is green and lovely with tender green foliage springing up.

As you look at the barren desert surrounding

the parched, dry riverbed, you wonder, "How could this little strip of land be green year round?" The answer lies in the fact that somewhere below the ground THE RIVER IS STILL FLOWING! There's a subterranean area far beneath the earth that's teeming with life! And even though we can't see the waters rippling along the surface, gushing and plunging toward the sea, the river is still flowing, and the vegetation along the riverbanks is making a powerful connection with that mighty river deep below the surface of the earth!

As I lay there, wanting to pray so badly I could taste it, the scripture in John 7:38 suddenly leaped out at me, where Jesus said, "Out of your belly [that subterranean area of your spirit] shall flow rivers of living water," and I knew that deep within me there was a subterranean area that was full of the Holy Ghost!

All at once, with this human frame lying at the very edge of death, I began moving my lips and I felt that mighty river flowing in the subterranean area of my belly. And in the next instant, I was praying in tongues under my breath! Had you been there in the room with me that night, you would have seen my lips moving even though I never uttered a sound. But I knew the Lord was hearing my prayer, for when you pray in tongues, you pray directly TO God, not to men. (See I Corinthians 14:2.)

At first, I could only pray from my chin up and

from my neck up, but I hung on with all the grit and determination I could muster because I wanted to dive down deeper into the waters, to get all the way down to that place where a mighty river was flowing! And, oh, what a great lesson I learned that night! And that is really what this whole book is all about.

> **YOU AND I MUST LEARN TO PRAY
> FROM THE RIVER WITHIN US,
> -- NOT FROM THE NECK UP
> AND NOT FROM THE LIPS.
> WE'VE GOT TO GET DOWN
> DEEP INTO THE RIVER,
> INTO THAT SUBTERRANEAN AREA,
> BECAUSE THE RIVER IS FLOWING!
> A MIGHTY RIVER IS FLOWING
> DAY AND NIGHT, 24 HOURS A DAY,
> SEVEN DAYS A WEEK,
> REACHING ALL THE WAY
> UP TO HEAVEN IN SPIRITUAL
> COMMUNICATION WITH GOD!**

Glory be to the Lord, there was a river of the Spirit flowing, flowing, flowing, even in that dark and lonely hospital room! When I began praying in tongues and plunged down deep into that subterranean area, I asked the Lord for the interpretation of my prayer, and gushing up out of my being came the words: *"YOU SHALL LIVE AND NOT DIE!"*

As I whispered those words over and over again under my breath, they were life to me! Like cool water in a barren desert, like a mother's hand on a fevered child at midnight, those words came to me as a rhema word from the Lord, bubbling up from that mighty subterranean river flowing through my belly area!

Early the next morning when Pastor Ralph Wilkerson came into my room, the first words that came out of his mouth were, "You shall live and not die."

Then my son Richard flew in from Tulsa and declared, "The Lord spoke to me and said that this is not unto death."

Later, Benny Hinn, Bill Swad, Dr. John Hagee, and several other great men of God came to lay their hands on me and pray for my healing, and one after the other confirmed the word God had given me — *"You shall live and not die!"*

IF WE'RE NOT CAREFUL, WE'LL OPERATE FROM THE MENTAL REALM ONLY AND NEVER CONNECT WITH THE RIVERS OF LIVING WATER

Friend, I want to share with you in the most intimate and personal way the real secret of what I learned through this earthshaking experience. *For*

*our praying to be effective, we've got to connect with
that subterranean area of our being where a mighty
river of God's Spirit is flowing.* For when the tongue
speaks by virtue of the mind's instruction only, it's
speaking by our intellect, which is a reasoning tool.
Our mind is argumentative, constantly reasoning,
and it often becomes entangled in an argument with
itself.

If we're not careful, we'll begin to operate from
the mental realm only, and it will submerge our
spirits and dominate us and we'll be Christians who
operate from the mouth out, from the chin up, from
the neck up. We'll never connect with that powerful
subterranean area of our spirits where the rivers of
living water are flowing!

As I prayed in the Spirit that night in my
hospital room, it was a resurrection experience far
greater than I can describe! And in spite of the
feeling of aloneness and the horrible fears that tried
to seize me, I received revelation, understanding,
and the word of the Lord came to me, **"You shall
live and not die!"** In the flash of a second, I grasped
how to pray! I could begin praying with my understanding, because my mind was now firmly an-
chored to the word of the Lord which came to me
through *praying in the Spirit with the interpretation!*

On one hand, I could have prayed in great
detail about the arrangements for my funeral. I
could have prayed that someone would say a few

good words over me and that my life would be deemed worthwhile.

On the other hand, I could pray for **LIFE MORE ABUNDANT** to surge through my 6'1"-tall, 175-pound body and that my heart would beat perfectly again so I could finish my ministry, breathing my last breath while I was praying for someone to be healed, in the mighty Name of Jesus and for His glory!

All at once, I could pray with my understanding. My previous understanding was marred by the questions, "Do I want to live? Do I want to die? Is life worth living like this? Do I have a message from Heaven about life?"

Oh, yes, I perceived the interpretation coming down from the Father Who had spoken from Heaven! The God Who talks had something to say to His servant, Oral Roberts: *"You shall live and not die!"* **Oh, hallelujah, I didn't have to pray death! I could pray LIFE, and** *life more abundant!*

There in that little room with my lips moving silently, I was praying up a storm under my breath until I prayed myself into a Holy Ghost release, a Holy Ghost shout! All of a sudden, it was like a light flashed in my spirit, and I got back into God's supernatural tracking system!

Then I became aware of something extraordinary happening in my body. It was like a warm liquid flowing through me, and I knew it was the

Spirit of God adding to the phenomenal work of the medical care professionals at Hoag Hospital who brought me back from the throes of death itself.

Almost immediately, the doctors began to label my recovery "remarkable," and I'll never forget the hour when they gave me the final treadmill test. Have you ever had one of those? Well, you run until you can't run anymore, and then the doctor asks you, "Can you run 15 more seconds?" So you run 30 seconds, and he asks, "Can you run 10 more seconds?" And he just keeps on prodding you to run until there's no breath left in your body!

After that test was finished, the doctor exclaimed, "This is the final test! The scar on your heart is HEALED! Your arteries are completely open, and you can do whatever you want to do!" Glory be to God, I can testify that the Lord has made my feet like hinds' feet, and He has set me upon my high places!

Friend, no matter what the upset has been in your life, or may be in the future, **OUR GOD IS STILL IN THE BUSINESS OF MAKING HIS CHILDREN'S FEET LIKE HINDS' FEET AND SETTING US IN OUR HIGH PLACES!** And He's setting us there through His supernatural tracking system of *praying in the Spirit with the understanding!*

You see, when you believe in Jesus, when you become a child of God, the Holy Spirit, Who brooded

143

over the face of the chaotic deep before this earth was formed, comes and fills you. He lives in your spirit, praying 24 hours a day on a straight line to glory, in wild abandon, going all out over the ledges of that great precipice between us and Heaven!

When our spirits are supernaturally tracking with the Lord, we can look up at those lofty heights, those dream goals on the horizon of life, and know that this is truly where our hiding place is from the devil and the perils of this wicked world.

We can strike out toward those high places with complete confidence, no longer paralyzed by the fear that we'll stumble and plunge to our death in the valley below us. There's a rock-solid assurance deep in our hearts that our feet are tracking with the Lord, so we can leap over those narrow ledges and harsh precipices with wild abandon, going all out for God, soaring higher and higher in Him, ***reaching all the way up to the place where He sets us . . . TO OUR HIGH PLACES IN HIM!***

Chapter 11

LIKE A MIGHTY RIVER FLOWING

The Lord has moved upon me to tell you one final story, and I believe it will pave the way for us to pray together concerning the prayer language of the Spirit!

Several years ago I met a man who was a building contractor, the head of his own large construction company, and he told me he had never heard of this marvelous experience of the Holy Spirit and what it could mean in his life. Then he attended a Full Gospel Business Men's Convention, founded by our dear friend, Demos Shakarian, and he was given the priceless opportunity to release the prayer language of the Spirit.

When he began to speak with tongues, he said he felt the most wonderful feeling of vitality and enthusiasm for the Lord and a tremendous release of power! And, later, his three sons, ages 14, 16, and 18, all received the same Holy Ghost power in their lives.

I'll never forget what that man told me after

receiving this glorious experience from the Lord.

> **HE DECLARED, "BROTHER ROBERTS, I HAD NEVER GRASPED WHAT SPIRITUAL POWER REALLY WAS UNTIL I DISCOVERED THE POWER OF THE HOLY SPIRIT IN MY LIFE!"**

And then he confided to me, "Now it's my driving goal to help everyone I know to receive this incredible power from the Lord!" And that's my goal, too, friend, because I know what an indescribable benefit *the prayer language of the Spirit with the interpretation* has been to me in my own life.

One of the most soul-satisfying things in the world is to pray directly to God, not to men, not for other people to hear you, but to pray to the Lord through this wonderful language that only God understands. This is especially precious when you're facing a problem that you haven't been able to climb over or you're wrestling with some great trial in your life.

When you pray in the Spirit, you don't have to turn your face up to the heavens and wonder how you're ever going to get through to the Lord over there beyond the stars! <u>When you pray in your prayer language, your prayer rushes straight through to God in that heavenly realm!</u> Oh, the beauty of the prayer language of the Spirit! It's a glorious experience and the Bible tells us to forbid it not! (See I Corinthians 14:39.)

You may say, "Oral, I want this Holy Ghost power in my life, but I don't know how to release my prayer language." Well, the most important step is to make Jesus Christ your Lord, because what God wants more than anything else is for you to cling to Him as the Savior of your life! If you haven't done it already, then this is your hour to open up your heart to God and tell Him how sorry you are that you've lived away from Him.

Or perhaps you once knew the Lord, but now you've gotten cold in your heart. Oh, it's the sweetest thing in the world to know that you know that you know that you belong to God! You can come alive in Him right now and receive a word from Heaven and a plan for your life! Just let the saving grace of Jesus Christ transform you as you pray this prayer out loud!

Lord God, be merciful to me, a human being who desperately needs Your help. I ask You for Your help, for divine power to enable me to choose this day Whom I will serve. I want to know You as my Savior, to be filled with God and with Your mighty Spirit. Come into my heart and forgive me of my sins. Save my soul and give me a brand-new birth.

Lord, I believe You have supernatural power to heal me, to uplift me, to take out all the hurt, the

disease, the bitterness and torment. Flood my soul
with joy and peace and make me a child of God who
really makes a difference!

In the Name of Christ I confess that Jesus is
my Lord. Oh, how He loved me, because He gave His
life for me! Help me to love Him with all of my being!
May Jesus Christ become so real in my soul that I will
know that I'm saved and that the Spirit of God has
taken possession of my life! I thank You for it, Lord!
Amen and amen.

Glory be to God! If you prayed that prayer
from your heart, you're now a child of God, born
again by His Spirit, and the power of the Lord is all
over you, from your head to your feet! Remember,
Jesus Himself said, "HE THAT BELIEVETH ON ME,
AS THE SCRIPTURE HATH SAID, OUT OF HIS
BELLY SHALL FLOW RIVERS OF LIVING WATER."
And then the Bible goes on to say, **"But this spake
he of the Spirit, which they that believe on him
should receive"** (John 7:38,39).

And I remind you of that great story in the
tenth chapter of the book of Acts, where the Apostle
Peter was preaching at the house of Cornelius and,
right in the midst of his sermon, Cornelius and his
entire household believed on the Lord Jesus Christ
as their personal Savior. The Bible says that THE
HOLY GHOST FELL ON THEM WHILE THEY STILL
HEARD THE WORD, and they spoke with tongues
and magnified God!

> ## MY FRIEND, YOU DON'T HAVE TO WRESTLE WITH THE LORD TO RECEIVE THE POWER OF THE HOLY SPIRIT!

You don't have to seek Him so desperately that you wear your body out and discourage your soul! I believe if you'll begin to tune in to God's Spirit this very moment, you'll feel something bubbling up within you. My brother, my sister, young person, *that's the Holy Ghost trying to break through.* **So why don't you let Him start flowing through your being right now!**

THE HOLY SPIRIT IS LIKE A RIVER

Jesus said that out of your belly, your inner-most being, shall flow RIVERS of living water. And let me tell you something very important about rivers. A river usually originates up in the mountains as a little spring running deep within the earth. Then it begins to sing and gurgle and splash along until finally it comes bubbling up to the surface. Before too long, it begins to rush downstream, swelling and overflowing its banks until at last it forms a great river channel. Then, as it swirls and races on toward the sea, it widens and deepens and becomes a mighty, rolling river!

Well, the Holy Spirit is like that, too! When the Lord comes in and cleanses you from sin, there's a river that starts flowing deep within you. It may be a little spring bubbling up in you at first, something you feel way down in the pit of your stomach. Then it begins to come welling up in you and, WHEN YOU YIELD TO IT, it becomes that **RIVER OF LIVING WATER** that the Lord declared would come rising up from your inner man! It's the Holy Spirit giving your spirit the power to speak in tongues, to release your prayer language, and to interpret back to your mind God's response. It's our talking God and you, a talking person, talking as if face-to-face! It starts in your will to do it.

Now some people say, "Oral, I thought God did it all," and I tell them, "Oh, God doesn't speak in tongues at all. PEOPLE SPEAK WITH TONGUES. *But the Holy Spirit gives them the words to speak.*" The Bible says in Acts 2:4, "They . . . began to speak with other tongues, *as the Spirit gave them utterance.*" And the Apostle Paul proclaimed, "I *WILL* pray with the spirit, and I *WILL* pray with the understanding also" (I Corinthians 14:15). That means releasing the prayer language of the Spirit is AN ACT OF YOUR HUMAN WILL. ***You must will to do it!***

I believe if you'll listen down in your spirit, you'll feel a sensation coming up from your innermost being of a sound or a syllable or a word that's not of an earthly language, but a heavenly one. Just begin to speak it out, and it won't be long until God will take those syllables and fashion them into a fluent PRAYER LANGUAGE OF THE SPIRIT. Then, as you listen for His response back to you, you'll begin to receive THE INTERPRETATION from the Lord.

Oh, it's the greatest honor in the world for me to pray for you to receive this glorious experience of the Holy Spirit's power! Somehow, in my spirit, I feel you're ready for it! So be bold! Ask the Lord for it! Expect God to give it to you! Hold your head up high, square your shoulders, open your mouth and expect the Lord to fill your mouth. I believe He'll give you the power of His Spirit, and my heart is bursting to pray for you right now:

O God, You declared in Your Holy Word that You are not so mysterious that You conceal Yourself from us, Your children. No, You said You've made the way so plain that even a wayfaring man or a little child could find You. That means, no matter how simple we are or how sophisticated, if we come to You, we can find You, and if we ask from You, **You said we will receive!**

And now, my friend, by the miraculous power of God upon my life, and through Jesus Christ of Nazareth, as His man of God, I pray that the Spirit of the Lord will begin to move through your being and lift you up to the realm of the miraculous! In the Name of Jesus, my Lord and Savior, I come against satan's opposition and every force that would hinder you from receiving ALL God has for your life!

By the Spirit of God living in me, I pray for you to <u>come into your divine destiny</u>, to be filled with the Holy Ghost and power! I pray that you'll rise up against satan! Stand up tall as a son or daughter of God, full of the Holy Ghost and power, and anointed by His Spirit from the crown of your head to the soles of your feet!

*Oh, my brother, my sister, the empowerment of your soul with the Holy Spirit is such a marvelous thing, and it's so important in your walk with God! I pray that you'll lift your hands to the Lord right now and say, "O God, I surrender my life to You. My heart's cry is to be full of Your Spirit, to speak with tongues and magnify God, and to interpret back to my mind -- my understanding -- and receive the divine revelations I need for my life. You said in Your Word that if I asked for bread, You would not give me a stone. (See Matthew 7:9-11.) So I expect to release my prayer language of the Spirit **and be a channel for Your miraculous power!** Amen."*

Now just stop and listen to the Spirit bubbling up inside you. Those are words that are coming, words of a heavenly language from God! Oh, don't be frightened. Just let them roll up out of your belly and over your tongue! Why don't you throw away all those barriers in your mind about the prayer language of the Spirit and LET IT FLOW! *Let it flood up out of your innermost being to God!*

And then begin to ask the Lord for the inter-pretation, for revelational knowledge to enter your spirit until you know that you know that you know that it's a word God is speaking inside your heart! I mean, expect to hear God inside yourself, a word coming down to you from Heaven above!

I'll tell you, when you receive from our Father according to the Bible, it's a glorious thing! It's wonderful beyond words! And if you want further prayer from one of our God-anointed, Holy Ghost-filled prayer partners, just step to your phone right now (918-495-7777), and let us know how we can help you **LIVE IN THE MIRACULOUS FLOW OF GOD!**

Remember, your prayer language of the Spirit, with the interpretation, is a mighty river flowing. It is living water. It is the glorified Lord Jesus Christ, sitting at the Father's right hand, receiving your believing and causing the Holy Spirit to be given to you as a mighty river flowing!

Let it flow in you!

I care about you!

I want to invite you to write to me. When you tell me what you're going through, I can know better how to write back to you . . . and how to pray and help you to believe God for A FLOW OF ABUNDANT MIRACLES to flood your life. *Simply fill out the Prayer Request Sheet* or address your personal letter to:

Oral Roberts
Tulsa, Oklahoma 74171

In Canada, write:
Oral Roberts
Toronto, Ontario M4P 2G2

When you write, I encourage you to consider planting a seed of your faith to God through this ministry. It's one of the best ways I know to help you release your faith to God and to look to Him alone to supply all your need according to Philippians 4:19.

PRAYER REQUEST SHEET

Brother Roberts,

     Please pray for the following prayer request(s):

_____

_____

_____

_____

_____

_____

_____

_____

_____

_____
Signature

☐ I would like to plant a Seed-Faith gift to God through your ministry. As I plant this seed of $_____, I believe God to multiply a harvest back to me in the area of my life where I need it the most.

Name_____

               (please print)   4501

Address _____

City _____

State _____ ZIP_____

Tear out this page and mail it to:
Oral Roberts, Tulsa, Oklahoma 74171

155

DON'T GIVE
THIS BOOK AWAY

Write me today and request another copy of UNLEASHING THE POWER OF PRAYING IN THE SPIRIT! for you to give to a friend or loved one. I'll send it to you free and postpaid for you to give to them personally.

Read UNLEASHING THE POWER OF PRAYING IN THE SPIRIT! often, at least a chapter each week from now on. Receive God's revelation on the prayer language of the Spirit, and learn how to pray in the Spirit with the understanding.

— — — — — — — — — — — — — — — — — — — —

Yes, I want to plant a seed and be made a blessing to someone else by giving them their own personal copy of UNLEASHING THE POWER OF PRAYING IN THE SPIRIT! Please rush another copy to me so I can help the person I have on my heart to receive the miracles they need.

Here is my Seed-Faith gift of $_____.

MY NAME_____
4500

ADDRESS_____

CITY_____ STATE _____ ZIP_____

Mail coupon to: Oral Roberts, Tulsa, Oklahoma 74171

When You Need Us...
We'll Be Here !

NEEDS can arise in your life any hour of any day.

Satan never lets up, but neither does the Abundant Life Prayer Group.

We're available to pray for your needs day or night, 24 hours a day, seven days a week.

And we're as close as your telephone. Call...

(918) 495-7777

Don't Miss A Miracle!

Watch *Miracles Now* with Oral and Richard Roberts every Sunday morning! Check your local lis